# CONCILIUM

*Religion in the Eighties*

*Concilium* 137 (7/1980): Church Order

# ELECTING OUR OWN BISHOPS

Edited by

**Peter Huizing**

and

**Knut Walf**

English Language Editor

Marcus Lefébure

**T. & T. CLARK**
Edinburgh

**THE SEABURY PRESS**
New York

September 1980
T. & T. Clark Ltd., 36 George Street, Edinburgh EH2 2LQ
ISBN: 0 567 30017 X

The Seabury Press, 815 Second Avenue, New York, N.Y. 10017
ISBN: 0 8164 2279 6

Library of Congress Catalog Card No.: 80 50584

Printed in Scotland by William Blackwood & Sons Ltd., Edinburgh

*Concilium:* Monthly except July and August.
Subscriptions 1980: All countries (except U.S.A. and Canada) £23·00 postage and handling included; U.S.A. and Canada $54.00 postage and handling included. (Second class postage licence 541-530 at New York, N.Y.) Subscription distribution in U.S. by Expediters of the Printed Word Ltd., 527 Madison Avenue, Suite 1217, New York, N.Y. 10022.

# CONTENTS

## Part III
### Ecclesial Organisation

## Part IV
### Bulletins

# Editorial

THE APPOINTMENT of men who are, by consecration, to receive the sacramental mission to the central government of a local church is one of the most fundamental problems of the renewal of structures in the Roman Catholic Church today. The tension that so often exists between the central government of that Church and its local churches is most clearly manifested in this problem of appointments.

We are confronted by these undeniable historical facts. One of the fundamental laws of Christianity in the first three centuries was that the local community, both 'clergy and people', had the right to choose its own presidents or leaders. That right was respected by popes and was even confirmed by them, several times quite explicitly, as inviolable. As the result of certain developments that took place over several centuries, this fundamental principle of the Church's law was replaced by another, at least in the Latin Church. This later law was the popes had the right freely to appoint bishops. This right existed long before it was formally laid down in code of law for the Latin Church in 1917-1918.

The historical contributions to this issue of *Concilium* (Part I) provide an brief analysis of the causes of this development. The fact that the profane and social part on the one hand and the political and economic part on the other played by the Church's dioceses became more and more important from the time of the Emperor Constantine onwards is, of course, decisive in this development. The legal principle of the free right of the popes to nominate bishops developed in the conflict of interests between the 'people', who gradually became reduced to the princes and other powerful figures, the 'clergy', gradually reduced to the cathedral chapters, within which there were also frequent conflicts between the majority and the minority, who claimed to be the *sanior pars*, and the See of Rome. The medieval canonists gave a legal status to this development in their concept of the 'fullness of papal power'. This concept was defined at the First Vatican Council as the supreme and direct legal power over all the churches, shepherds and faithful, both together and separately.

Partly because of the new understanding of the Church that emerged at the Second Vatican Council, local churches, precisely as communities of believers, have in recent years come to think of themselves legally as independent legal subjects, in which the Church of Christ and his Spirit is made completely real and present. According to this understanding of the Church, the Church is a community of churches that are essentially equal in value. The churches of Antioch, Corinth or Philippi, for example, were in no way lesser churches and their members were in no way lesser members of the Church than the church of Rome and its members. In that community of churches, the basis of the legal relationships is the independent legal subjectivity of each church, together with the legal consequences with regard to that church's independent authority to act that are connected with that legal subjectivity. The coordinating leadership of that community is the task of the college of bishops and that college is subject to the leadership of the bishop of Rome.

The fullness of power, defined, as we have seen, by the First Vatican Council as the supreme and direct legal power over all the churches, shepherds and faithful and ascribed by both the medieval canonists and the Fathers of the Council to the bishop of Rome, does not exist in a vacuum. This power or authority is essentially and from within related to the independent legal subjectivity of the churches and the second is just as much essentially and from within related to the first. If one of the two poles is made absolute, then one or other right is violated and the very possibility that right may exist in the Roman Catholic Church is also denied. Even if we do not go quite so far as to make one of these two poles absolute, it is still true to say that even a disturbance of the proper balance between the two poles will cause a disturbance in the entire legal order of the Church.

Assuming that independent legal subjectivity and the right of local churches to self-determination within the community of all the churches are firm data, we may say that one clear consequence of this is that those churches have a right to be consulted about and to influence the appointment of the men who are to be entrusted with the central government of the same churches (see the first two articles in Part II). This does not have to be a right to a completely autonomous choice of those leaders by 'clergy and people', as was the case in the earliest Christian communities. This would, in any case, hardly be possible to achieve in the present structure of the Church's dioceses and their mutual communications. A legal structure for the appointment of bishops ought now to preserve a correct balance between the various bodies that are directly involved, in other words, between the clergy and people of the diocese concerned, the Church province or college of bishops concerned and the See of Rome.

An initial attempt to give a rather more prominent position to the people in the appointment of a bishop was made in the new liturgy of the consecration of a bishop (see the third article in Part II). In this liturgy, the people are once again more actively involved and the local church asks the new bishop's predecessor to consecrate this priest as a bishop. The pope's letter nominating the bishop is then read out. The author of this article comments that this action in the liturgy is meaningless if the local church has played no part in the nomination and is even less meaningful if the new bishop has been imposed on that church against its will.

The author of the contribution on the present law and the draft of the revised law governing the appointment of bishops concludes that both the old and the new laws far from satisfy the desire that the whole people of God should collaborate in the filling of the Church's offices and the desire for a re-introduction of choice in appointing bishops. This is in spite of the fact that these desires go back directly to the renewed understanding of the Church that emerged at the Second Vatican Council and that Council's explicit teaching about the participation of all members of the Church in the threefold office of Christ and the fundamental equality of all the baptised (see the first article in Part III).

It would, however, not be enough simply to promulgate a new law that provided in theory for an equal participation of all those concerned in the appointment of a bishop, so long as the present gulf between the legal and political procedure in use in the Church on the one hand and the liturgical celebration of the sacramental consecration of a bishop on the other continues to exist. This whole procedure must be directed towards the action that really makes a man a bishop. This action should not be taken in the name of the pope, the college of bishops or the whole people of God—it is an action in the name of Christ. A social psychologist has therefore suggested in his contribution to this issue of *Concilium* that the principle of the participation of the clergy and people should be applied to this whole procedure. In other words, the procedure ought to take place in the religious sphere of 'prayer and fasting' if it is to be effectively removed from the secular and political sphere of influence (see the third article in Part III).

It is not essential for each individual taking part in the procedure to have a good intention. A good intention can be presupposed so long as it is not obvious that the procedure is dominated by a bad intention. What is essential is that the whole procedure should have a clearly religious character, an unmistakably symbolic value for the community of believers, who will recognise that it is inspired by faith.

*Translated by David Smith*

PETER HUIZING
KNUT WALF

# PART I

*History*

PART I

Peter Stockmeier

# The Election of Bishops by Clergy and People in the Early Church

SCHOLARS are wont to invoke the idea of 'evolution' to explain and even legitimise the changing face of early Christianity, which is thus viewed—to continue the biological analogy—as little more than a phenotype of the Church of today. In this perspective an inquiry into the way bishops were appointed in the early Church can be of purely antiquarian interest. Three factors, however, have combined to intensify popular interest in the problems associated with this issue: the shortcomings apparent in the centralised administration of the contemporary Roman Catholic Church; the enhanced status of the episcopal office in the wake of the Second Vatican Council; and the newly awakened self-assertion of Catholic believers. As a result of these impulses the pope's freedom to appoint bishops—notwithstanding the many variations between the respective Concordats—no longer appears as the unsurpassable high-water mark of historical development; rather, it appears as a time-conditioned product of this development and hence as something capable of appropriate improvement. A correct 'theology of office' does not necessarily entail the immersion of administrative procedures in a cloud of mystery. The question of the election of bishops has unfortunately been too closely bound up with the debate about the democratisation of the Church with the result that, although the latter has shown signs of flagging of late, the former has incurred guilt by association.[1] It would of course be methodologically impermissible to short-circuit discussion of this topic by interpreting the texts which speak of the popular election of bishops in terms of the democratic notion that the people are the source of all authority. Nor may we go to the opposite extreme of justifying a dominant practice by the shoddy device of spiritualising away or even outrightly ignoring the relevant evidence.

Our survey of this issue will begin by considering the New Testament references to the appointment of office-bearers. We shall then trace the various types of episcopal election which developed in the first centuries, bringing this article to a close with a discussion of the post-Constantinian era. It is to be noted in advance that we intend neither to give a clear-cut description of the function of a bishop nor to offer a general account of the theology of office.[2]

3

## 1. THE RESPONSIBILITY OF THE CONGREGATION ACCORDING TO THE NEW TESTAMENT

The conspicuous absence from the New Testament writings of the office of bishop as is materialised in the course of the second century is sufficient proof of the variety which characterised the developing outward structure of the Church. Such variety was likewise displayed in the procedure whereby individual believers were called to serve the Church. While it is clear that Jesus himself was responsible for the call of the Twelve, no fixed principle is discernible in the appointment of office-bearers in the ensuing period. On the contrary, this took place in different ways. Hence it would surely seem that the young Church possessed no clear-cut orders from Jesus himself on this subject.

Already in the 'by-election' to fill the place among the Twelve forfeited by Judas (Acts 1:15-26) the 120 brethren propose two suitable candidates: 'And they cast lots for them, and the lot fell on Matthias' (Acts 1:26). Casting lots was looked on as an ancient mode of ascertaining the divine will; and since it was a customary feature of the temple service in Jerusalem this procedure cannot be regarded as a specifically Christian method of appointment. It is obvious in this case that the whole community of the disciples took part in nominating a replacement who must be a witness of the life and death of Jesus.

According to Acts 6:1-7 the so-called deacons were likewise chosen by all the disciples, and the sole prerequisite for candidacy was possession of the Holy Spirit and wisdom. Suitability on the one hand and election by the assembly on the other led to the setting apart of individual members of the Church on whom the Apostles then laid hands. The word for 'choose' occurs frequently in the New Testament in the sense of God's gracious election, which implies the operation of the Holy Spirit.[3] This dimension is not excluded in the case of election by the congregation, nor does it diminish the significance of the concrete congregation as an electoral body.

Finally, it was in concert with the Apostles and presbyters that 'the whole church' brought the so-called Apostolic Council to an end by choosing envoys to send to Antioch. On this occasion, though, the laity would seem to have played a subordinate role (Acts 15:22-29). The joint responsibility of the Church as a whole can of course also be discharged by individual members, as when according to Acts 13:1ff the 'prophets and teachers' at Antioch chose Barnabas and Paul for missionary service under the direct influence of the Holy Spirit (and see I Tim. 1:18; 4:14). And according to Acts 14:23 these two missionaries appointed presbyters for their converts, a procedure which is also attended in Tit. 1:5.

Thus the New Testament data offer no unified description of the appointment of office-bearers in the churches, unless we detect such unity in the fact that bishops are usually mentioned in the plural (see Phil. 1:1; Acts 20:28). The relevant texts more than once specify the congregation as being actively involved in the choice of its ministers. Although we cannot define its function more precisely, we can still sense congregational participation even in those cases where the laity do not appear as the sole component of the electoral college. Hence the people *qua* church bear a share of the responsibility for the appointment of office-bearers, and the designation of this procedure as 'pneumatic' (L. Goppelt) does nothing to alter the fact that the people themselves elect their leaders, an act of the people of God to which ordination corresponds.

## 2. THE APPOINTMENT OF BISHOPS IN THE PRE-CONSTANTINIAN ERA

In virtue of the non-occurrence of the Parousia, special importance was attached to ecclesiastical offices since their bearers were regarded as guarantors of tradition. This is especially true of the monarchical episcopate which makes its first appearance in the letters of Ignatius (themselves perhaps to be dated as late in the middle of the second century). The idea of the minister as guarantor of tradition finds a striking expression in the letter of the Roman church to Corinth at the end of the first century. The author develops a consistent model of succession (I Clement 42), the theological objective of which is not, however, in full accord with the New Testament. Irenaeus of Lyons (d. circa 200) used this combination of the principles of tradition and succession to argue against the Gnostic heresies,[4] thereby helping to propagate the historically unfounded notion that the transmission of the truth is dependent on the successor's being appointed directly to the episcopal chair by his predecessor. Given that the tradition-oriented model of succession tended to influence the way men thought of the actual appointment of office-bearers, it is truly remarkable that the role of the congregation in this matter does not pass unmentioned in the Letter of Clement. Denouncing the unlawfulness of the action taken against the presbyters in Corinth, I Clem. 44:3 states that they were appointed by the Apostles or by men of good standing 'with the consent of the whole Church'. While the text as a whole is strongly redolent of 'the manner of Hellenistic officialdom',[5] it presupposes congregational participation in the choice of office-bearers as a familiar custom, making no attempt to suppress knowledge of this fact despite its own stress on the idea of institutional succession. Hence I Clement continues a practice which we have already encountered in the New Testament witnesses and which will largely prevail in the ensuing period. The intervention of the Roman church in a question pertaining to the ministerial office is, moreover, in keeping with our interpretation.

The appeal made in the fifteenth chapter of the Didache seems to be a fundamental injunction rather than simply a casual remark: 'You must, then, elect for yourselves bishops and deacons who are a credit to the Lord, men who are gentle, generous, faithful, and well tried. For their ministry to you is identical with that of the prophets and teachers.'[6] The correct performance of the divine worship mentioned in the previous chapter obviously requires suitable superintendents, men who have taken the place of the charismatic prophets and teachers, having attained this position by election. According to this instruction it is not appointment by existing office-bearers but the people's choice—made, admittedly, in accordance with specific criteria—which calls a man into the service of bishop and deacon. Hence the Didache proves that in the Syria and Palestine of the second century election 'from below' claimed a kind of equality with the endowment of the Spirit 'from above'.

The Apostolic Tradition written by Hippolytus in Rome around A.D. 215 expressly emphasises the election of bishops by the whole people: 'Let the bishop be ordained after he has been chosen by all the people.'[7] Since earlier liturgical traditions are described in other parts of this Church order, it can safely be assumed that Hippolytus here reproduces the familiar practice of the Roman church with respect to the appointment of bishops. While the insistent command that all the people have to elect the bishop can be read as indicating the existence of local tensions on this score, the remark certainly underlines the fact that the electoral proceedings are the concern of the whole church. As is well known, this provision found a place in the so-called Apostolic Constitutions, which invoke apostolic authority in their prescription that 'a man be consecrated bishop who is blameless in every respect and who is elected by the people'.[8] Since we are dealing here with the largest anthology of ancient canon law, there is no reason to doubt the universal validity of this rule, although at the time of its formulation (circa A.D. 360) misgivings had long been registered about the appropriateness of this electoral procedure. It is therefore all the more striking that the pseudo-apostolic author of this legal anthology declares the election of bishops by the people to be a divine command, thereby precluding any gloss which might advocate the direct appointment of bishops without reference to the people.

If we return for a moment to the pre-Constantinian period we find that the letters of Cyprian of Carthage (d. 258) furnish a vivid picture of the state of affairs in the Latin Church. While this pastor is an early example of the emergence of a pronounced episcopal and hierarchical self-consciousness, this tendency did not lead him to play down the responsibility of the laity to appoint church leaders. The account given in his biography of Cyprian's withdrawal in humility 'when the whole people rose up in love and honour for him under the inspiration of the Lord'[9] may be a hagiographical topos, but it can only produce the desired effect on the reader if the people actually took part in the election of their bishops. This sharing of responsibility is in keeping with the ancient Church's custom of resolving the problems which beset it by way of mutual consultation. Cyprian comments on this custom as follows: 'It accords with everyone's modesty, discipline and conduct for us overseers (bishops), meeting together with the clergy and in the presence of the steadfast people who themselves deserve honour for their faith and their fear of God, to be able conscientiously to dispose all things by mutual consultation.'[10] In the context of the question under discussion, namely the readmission to communion of those who have denied the faith under persecution, the principle of mutual consultation sheds light on the typical procedures of early Christian churches. Even so, it puts some difficulties in the way of a more precise definition of the people's actual role in the appointment of bishops. Does Cyprian mean that the people truly exercise their right of election, or that they can merely acclaim the successful candidate, or that they simply constitute a public forum in virtue of their attendance at the event?

An examination of the pertinent references in his letters shows that Cyprian probably speaks of an active participation by the people. Now the Numidian bishop Antonianus had received a one-sided account of the elevation of Pope Cornelius (251-253) from the Roman presbytery Novatian. Cyprian therefore wrote to his brother-bishop as follows: 'But Cornelius was made bishop by the judgment (*iudicium*) of God and of his Christ, by the testimony (*testimonium*) of almost all the clergy, by the vote (*suffragium*) of the people then present, and with the approbation of long-serving priests and of upright men, and all this at a time when no one else had been made bishop before him and when the place of Fabianus—that is, of Peter—and the dignity of the sacerdotal chair was still unfilled.'[11] Cyprian describes the active participation of the Roman laity in the appointment of Cornelius as *suffragium*, hence with the word used to denote the citizens' voting in the *comitia*.[12] And the function of the clergy is characterised as *testimonium*, probably under the influence of the term employed in the Roman code of legal procedure for evidence given out of court.[13] Since the subject of this whole section is the legality of Cornelius' elevation, we may detect in Cyprian's mention of the *iudicium Dei*, the *testimonium* of the clergy, the *suffragium* of the people and the approbation of long-serving priests those elements of a correct appointment which were regarded as of decisive importance. But that we cannot deduce a clear-cut procedure from these legal concepts is proved by Cyprian's account of the election of the Spanish bishop Sabinus. According to this report it is to be reckoned as divine tradition and apostolic custom that the bishops of the province and the people of the diocese come together to institute a bishop according to law (*ordinationem iure perfectam*) 'in virtue of the vote of the whole brotherhood and of the judgment of the bishops'.[14] Here too unequivocal emphasis is given to the essential role of the people and the whole process is represented as something involving the whole Church. It is of course God who ultimately ratifies the appointment of the bishop-elect.

The evidence which we have adduced from the first centuries proves that people and clergy had an essential part to play in the appointment of a bishop. While this joint responsibility could take various forms, congregational franchise unquestionably held the foremost place, even though other modes of regulating the succession—of which an extreme example is furnished by the transmission of the episcopal office by heredity[15]—existed alongside it. In such cases the role of the people may occasionally have been restricted to acclaiming the bishop-elect. The frequent attestation of elections, however, argues for the view that the appointment of bishops usually took place in this way, a fact which the Historia Augusta significantly mentions as a model for the appointment of government officials.[16]

### 3. THE APPOINTMENT OF BISHOPS IN THE POST-CONSTANTINIAN ERA

With the recognition of Christianity by the State under the Emperor Constantine the Great (306-337) and the increasing integration of Church and State during the ensuing period, the episcopal office was caught in a public conflict of interests which did not remain without consequences for the method of appointing ecclesiastical office-bearers. The interests of the Church were increasingly invested with political importance, thus provoking intervention on the part of the State. A distinct but complementary factor was the growing prestige of the episcopal office, which was therefore soon coveted by members of the upper classes.

In spite of this change even the post-Constantinian Church developed no clear-cut legal norms in accordance with which Church leaders should be appointed. The practice of bishops being elected by people and clergy seems to have continued, although it underwent strong modifications in the direction of an increased episcopal influence. The Council of Arles (314) already laid stress on the role of the bishops with its decree forbidding a bishop to act independently in the consecration of his successor.[17] This Council, however, is untypical in making no mention of the influence of the laity, which was so extensive at this time that a bishop could be appointed to a diocese and yet not be accepted by it. This was laid down in the eighteenth canon of the Council of Ancyra (314), which thus took the side of the congregation, directing the bishop-elect to return to his former parish.[18] Finally, the important fourth canon of the Ecumenical Council of Nicaea enjoined that a bishop should in principle be installed by all his episcopal colleagues in the same eparchy.[19] Since this requirement was not met when he was elevated to the bishopric of Alexandria in 328, Athanasius did not neglect in his justification of this procedure to point out the vigorous participation of the people.[20] In the wake of the Donatist debates and of the Arian disorders the installation of bishops won a significance which often transcended the interests of a local church. It is therefore understandable that the role of the bishops came to the fore in the pertinent regulations.

Yet even at this time, as the above-mentioned Apostolic Constitutions demonstrate, the people continued to play an active part in choosing their bishop. It was possible for the people spontaneously to proclaim a man bishop, as happened in the case of Ambrose.[21] The vote of clergy and people manifestly remained an integral element of the appointment even when, as in Gaul, the role of the metropolitans came increasingly to the fore.[22] In an admonitory letter to Gaul occasioned by the removal from office of a sick bishop, Pope Leo the Great (440-461) hearkened back to older Roman norms: 'At the very least let no action be taken until the citizens have voted and the people given their testimony. And let the opinion of respected men be sought, along with the choice of the clerics. For these practices are customarily observed in the ordination of bishops (*sacerdotes*) by those who are acquainted with the rules of the fathers.'[23] Thus even Pope Leo I, who gave such forceful expression to his consciousness of the papal primacy, depicted the election of bishops by clergy and people as the traditional law of the Church. According to him the metropolitan ought only to intervene in the event of malpractices.[24]

It is significant that the franchise of clergy and people was more likely to remain in use in the Western than in the Eastern Church, where many commentators were disposed to interpret the provisions of Nicaea as a decision in favour of episcopal jurisdiction. The growing number of malpractices was largely responsible for the restrictions which came to be placed on popular election. Ambrose wholeheartedly advocated cooperation between the believers concerned and the bishops of the province in the matter of episcopal appointments, but he warned at the same time against the intrusion of 'human covetousness' in this sphere.[25] And at this period the electoral process itself had already fallen into discredit under the influence of group interests, so that it was no longer able to guarantee that the worthiest man was called to the episcopal office.[26] John Chrysostom (d. 407), whose own preferment to the chair of Constantinople owed much to imperial intrigue, complained bitterly about his unwholesome state of affairs: 'All those who are qualified to confer the honoured office split into many parties, and one can observe how the assembled presbyters agree neither among themselves nor with the one to whom the episcopal dignity has fallen. Everyone clings to his own viewpoint in that one votes for this candidate and another for that.'[27] This observation, to which there are many parallels, affirms that a variety of interests were at work in the episcopal appointments of late antiquity. Restriction of the franchise of people and clergy was prominent among the means whereby an attempt was made to remedy this state of affairs.

A survey of the history of official appointments in the early Church demonstrates that bishops were undoubtedly elected by clergy and people from the beginning. Even though this participation took a variety of forms, the role of the people cannot be reduced simply to one of acclamation. The significance of this finding is emphatically not that an ecclesiastical office is conferred 'from below'; rather, the operation of the Holy Spirit is expressed in the decision of the Church. Sadly, the increasing entanglement of believers in the concerns and trends of the society of late antiquity led to malpractices which churchmen sought to eliminate by tying episcopal appointments more closely to ecclesiastical norms and to their guarantors in the hierarchy.

*Translated by John Stephenson*

## Notes

1. Some years ago J. Ratzinger referred to the ostensible identity of the sociological concept of a 'people' with the 'people of God'. He maintained that the latter is distinguished from the former by a 'spiritual transposition'. See 'Demokratisierung der Kirche' J. Ratzinger and J. Maier, eds *Demokratie in der Kirche. Möglichkeiten, Grenzen, Gefahren (Werdende Welt* 16) (Limburg 1970) 9-46, at 27-29.

2. On this topic see C. J. von Hefele 'Die Bischofswahlen in den ersten christlichen Jahrhunderten (*Beiträge zur Kirchengeschichte, Archäologie und Liturgik* I) (Tübingen 1864) 140-144; F. X. Funk *Bischofswahlen im christlichen Altertum und im Anfang des Mittelalters (Kirchengeschichtliche Abhandlungen und Untersuchungen* I) (Paderborn 1897) pp. 23-39; K. Müller 'Die älteste Bischofswahl und-weihe in Rom und Alexandrien' *ZNW* 28 (1929) 274-296; F. L. Ganshof 'Note sur l'élection des évêques dans l'empire romain au IVme et pendant la première moitié du Vme siècle'*Rev. intern. des droits de l'antiquité* (1950) 467-498; P. Stockmeier 'Gemeinde und Bischofsamt in der alten Kirche' *TThQ* 149 (1969) 133-146; R. Gryson 'Les élections ecclésiastiques au IIIme siècle' *RHE* 68 (1973) 353-404.

3. See G. Schrenk and G. Quell 'ἐκλέγομαι κτλ' *ThWNT* IV pp. 147-197, esp. p. 179.

4. See Irenaeus *Adv. haer.* III 3, 1 (*Harvey* II 8sq.).

5. R. Knopf *Lehre der zwölf Apostel. Zwei Clemensbriefe (Handbuch zum Neuen Testament* companion volume I) (Tübingen 1920) p. 119.

6. Bihlmeyer-Schneemelcher p. 8. (Quoted here from *Library of Christian Classics* I, p. 178). See R. Knopf *Lehre der zwölf Apostel* p. 37.

7. *Trad. apost.* 2 (*Botte* 4). (Quoted here from *The Apostolic Tradition of Hippolytus* tr. B. S. Easton Cambridge 1934 p. 33).

8. *Const. Apost.* VIII 4, 2 (*Funk* I p. 473).

9. Pontius *Vita Cypriani* 5 (*CSEL* III III p. XCV lines 15-16).

10. Cyprian *Ep.* 19, 2 (*CSEL* III II p. 526 lines 4-8).

11. Cyprian *Ep.* 55, 8 (*CSEL* III II p. 629 21-p. 630 2).

12. Cf. K. Kübler 'Suffragium' *Pauly-Wissowa* II 4, 1 654-658.

13. See M. Kaser *Das römische Zivilprozessrecht* (*Handbuch der Altertumswissenschaften* III 4) (Munich 1966) pp. 281-283.

14. Cyprian *Ep.* 67, 5 (*CSEL* III II p. 739 lines 15-17).

15. See the complaints voiced by Origen in *Hom. in Num* 22, 4 (*GCS* 7 208 26).

16. *Vita Alexandri Severi* 45, 6 sq. (*Samberger-Seyfarth* I p. 287).

17. C. J. von Hefele *Conciliengeschichte* I 2nd ed. (Freiburg 1873) p. 215. On the general developments, see J. Gaudemet *L'Église dans l'Empire romain* (*Histoire du Droit et des Institutions de l'Église en Occident* III) (Paris 1958) pp. 330-341.

18. C. J. von Hefele *Conciliengeschichte* p. 237f.

19. *Ibid.* pp. 381-386.

20. Athanasius *Apol. c. Arian.* 6, 5 (*Opitz* p. 92).

21. Paulinus *Vita Ambr.* 6 (*PL* 14, 31 A).

22. Zosimus *EP.* 1 (*CSEL* 35 I p. 100f).

23. Leo *Ep.* 10, 4 (*PL* 54, 632).

24. Leo *Ep.* 14, 5 (*PL* 54, 673 A).

25. Ambrose *Ep.* 63, 48 (*PL* 16, 1273).

26. Gregory of Nazianzus speaks of 'those who have become theologians in virtue of a certain number of votes' in *Or.* 20, 1 (*PG* 35 1066 A); see Jerome *ad Jovin.* 1, 34 (*PL* 23, 269 C).

27. John Chrysostom *Sacerd.* 3, 15 (*PG* 48, 652).

B

# Jean Gaudemet

# Bishops:
# From Election to Nomination

THE STAGE was set by the declaration which Gratian made *a propos* of the designation of bishops (*Dist.* 62 and 63) in his Decretum towards the year 1140: 'The clergy is to elect, the people to consent' (the opening *dictum* of *Dist* 62). Eight centuries later, canon 329 §2 of the Code of Canon Law of 1917 affirmed: 'The Roman pontiff has full discretion to nominate bishops.'

The contrast between the two texts constitutes a stinging rejoinder to those who maintain that the Roman Church as guardian of Tradition never makes changes of discipline. This change challenges the historian: When did this serious change come about, and how and why?

We cannot here go into every historical and regional detail of the stages of this development, nor evoke the places which have not experienced it quite so sharply. The general direction is clear enough, the chronological framework agreed enough, to enable us to describe what happened in 'Christendom' as a whole, for it was in this medieval and Western Christendom that the mutation occurred.[1] In order to understand it, we need to begin by recalling the situation on the eve of the transformation which took less than two centuries to come about (between the last decades of the twelfth century and the first decades of the fourteenth). We shall then inquire into the causes, and finally bring out the main results of this development by way of a conclusions.

## 1. THE SITUATION ON THE EVE OF THE CHANGE

The old principle of election *a clero et populo* was frequently invoked in the course of the eleventh century and at the beginning of the twelfth century, whilst in practice the feudal lords, both great and small, only too often usurped the right to designate prelates.

The canonical collections of the eleventh century, and particularly the two *Decreta* of Burchard of Worms and Ivo of Chartres, which respectively open and close the century, recall the texts from which the time of the letters of St Leo to Rusticus of Narbonne in 458-459 or of Gelasius I in 494 and the Councils of the high Middle Ages had required that bishops be elected.

From the Merovingian epoch in Gaul, however, the kings wanted to dispose of bishoprics and in the disorder which marked the end of the Carolingian era secular rulers extended their grip to the dioceses (not sparing even Rome). 'Political' motives and family concerns were behind these ambitions. Bishops had become part and parcel of the feudal regime and had become territorial rulers as well as pastors, and so came to wield political power. The suzerains could not remain indifferent to such vassals. Quite apart from holding territorial and therefore political power in this way, however, the bishops also, of course, exercised an inherent influence on the mass of the faithful and so represented a force with which secular rulers had to reckon. And immediate material interests compounded such political considerations. The territorial wealth of bishoprics constituted a tempting means of securing close relatives or to remunerate services rendered. The control which the feudal lords exercised enabled them to satisfy their family and familiars. The designation to the bishopric of Rheims of, first, Arnoul, then of Gerbert, enforced by Hugh Capet for political reasons, the designation of Conrad as archbishop of Salzburg by the emperor in 1106, all show the importance which the princes attached to the choice of bishops and the way in which they assumed this control.

It was in order to combat such abuses that the 'Gregorian' reformers vigorously recalled the elective principle from the middle of the eleventh and towards the first half of the twelfth century. Already in 1016/1017 Fulbert of Chartres was writing: 'How can one speak of election where a person is imposed by the prince, so that neither clergy nor people, let alone the bishops, can envisage any other candidates.' In the middle of the century Humbert of Moyenmoutiers deplored the fact that 'in the election of bishops, kings come before primates and metropolitans. . . . The roles are reversed.'

The Council of Rheims of 1049, presided over by Leo IX, declared: 'Nobody should be promoted to government in the Church unless he has been elected by the clergy and the people' (Chap. 1). At the Synod of Rome of 7th March 1080, Gregory VII recalled that election by the clergy and people constituted the canonical method of designating prelates, and the Lateran Council of 1123, in an unequivocal formula, decided that 'nobody is to consecrate somebody who has not been elected canonically to the epis- copate'. The scandal of the designation by Philip I of the young Etienne de Garlande (at the age of twenty-two), son of the king's seneschal, as bishop of Beauvais, was roundly denounced in the celebrated letters of Ivo of Chartres. It would be easy enough, but rather profitless, to multiply such examples. The evil was widespread. Yet the energy and the patience of the 'Gregorians' triumphed over the worst excesses of secular imperialism. Through either formal agreements (Concordat of Worms) or the estab- lishment of *modus vivendi* (in France or England), the secular powers were obliged to renounce the brutal imposition of the candidates. In France the king retained the right to authorise the election and, by means of the mechanism of the restitution of temporal power to the prelate, to approve of (or refuse) the choice. We should, however, note that, with rate exceptions, the canonists defended the liberty of the Church by restoring the elective system rather than by appealing to a remote and sometimes lacklustre papacy. This is the regime to which the Decretum of Gratian bore witness towards 1140. In Distinctions 62 and 63 it recalled the elective principle at the same time as it attacked lay interference.

Lay intervention had taken two forms which were completely different but alike in their manifestation and in their motivation. From the first centuries onwards the community of clergy and laity had chosen its pastor on the simple ground that, as Pope Celestine I had put it in 428, 'no bishop ought to be imposed on those who do not want him'. On the other hand, since the Merovingian Age, kings, emperors and barons had disposed of bishoprics. Was the 'exclusion of the laity' aimed at the participation of the faithful or at the caprice of princes? The way in which the texts assembled by Gratian are intertwined with each other in Distinction 63 shows that both considerations preoc- cupied him. The imperious formulas which open Distinction 63 seems to be definitive: 'Layfolk should not meddle with an election in any way.' What the texts adduced to support this dogma in fact show is that it is above all a question of excluding the manoeuvres of the great to impose their candidates. This has to be seen as being in the wake of the 'Gregorian' effort to condemn the control of the princes and lords over the bishoprics. At the same time the participation of layfolk in the choice of pastors, within the context of the community of the faithful, is also involved. Not that the object here is wholly to exclude the laity but, in accordance with the scheme of *duo genera Christianorum* that was henceforth to become classical, to subordinate the laity to the *sacerdotes*. The declarations reinforce each other: 'The clergy is to elect, the people to consent' (the opening *dictum* of Distinction 62). Gratian quotes the formula of Celestine I in 429, 'The people must be taught, not followed', then comments: 'The people must not go ahead, but must follow' (*dictum* on Distinction 62, c. 2). At the same time, because he cannot omit the texts which affirm the rights of princes (Distinction 63, cc. 8-25), he concludes in a nuanced way (*dictum* after c. 25): 'It is clear that layfolk must not be excluded from an election and that princes must not be kept out. However, the fact that the people have a part to play in the election does not mean that it is called to conduct it; but it must give its consent to the election made by the clergy.'

There is scarcely any mention of pontifical intervention in the Decretum of Gratian.

## 2. THE CAUSES OF THE CHANGE

Two developments over less than two centuries came to disturb this regime: the contraction of the electoral college to the limits of the cathedral chapter, which tended to be torn by lively tensions, and the will of Rome.

(*a*) From the earliest time the electoral college had been analysed in a 'hierarchising' sense. Leo the Great distinguished 'the wishes of the citizens, popular testimony, the opinions of the notables, the election by the clergy' (*Epistola* 10, 4; 445) and accounts of elections show that the acclamations of the crowd only ratified a choice made by other means. We have already seen that Gratian sought to reduce the role of the laity. In their commentaries on his collection, the Decratalists of the twelfth century went further in the same direction: 'When the people gives its consent, it does no more than follow the way marked out by the clergy which votes' declared Etienne de Tournai towards 1160 (*Summa*, on Distinction 63). Alexander III completed the process in a letter to the Chapter of Bremen in 1180: 'Layfolk should not be admitted to vote.' This was a new attitude, as the *Summa Reginensis* underlined a little after 1191: 'The consent of layfolk is no longer solicited these days because their admission would occasion trouble in the election.' The same exclusion is to be found in the Council of Avignon in 1209 (Chap. 8) and above all in a decretal of Gregory IX (I, 6, 56).

Many even of the clergy were kept out. Thus for practical reasons only the clergy of the bishop's town, where the election was held, could take part in it. There would be few abbeys in the neighbourhood which had the means and the inclination to go to the town for that purpose, even though they might be in charge of a diocesan church. The chapter's monopoly became a fact and the reminder of the right of 'religious men' to take part in the election, formulated by the Lateran Council of 1139 (Chap. 28), soon became a dead letter.

Once the electoral college had become reduced to the cathedral chapter alone, it soon showed how ineffective it was. Peace did not always reign in this closed world and the election of a bishop was the occasion of confrontations which sometimes degenerated into battles. There may have been no rule compelling the election of a bishop from among the canons, but experience showed that they—and the arch-deacon in particular—were well placed to be candidates. Personal ambition and collegial rivalries combined to exploit the intricacies of the electoral procedure. The antithesis of number and quality, of the *maior pars* and the *sanior pars*, exacerbated the spirit of chicanery, since every minority might be defeated numerically but could well retort that it was the 'wiser' group. This is what gave rise to interminable conficts, of which the texts preserve innumerable traces. And the debates and proceedings which resulted prolonged the vacancy of the episcopal see to the great detriment of the diocese and the faithful.

Incapable of dominating their passions, the electors were obliged to turn to Rome and to ask the pope to arbitrate. In this way, they recognised their incapacity and offered the papacy the chance to take their place. For the pope (or a prelate commissioned by him) often settled the debate by imposing his own candidate. Examples of such designations are to be found from the pontificate of Gregory VII onwards. They remained very infrequent until the last decades of the twelfth century but became very common with Innocent III. Appeal against an objection to an elector was deemed to be a *causa maior*, to be decided by Rome alone. There are innumerable examples of such objections and Gregory X at the Council of Lyons in 1274 (Chap. 9) tried to check their 'unbridled frequency'. Further, in order to avoid overlong vacancies or the confirmation of unworthy candidates, the Fourth Lateran Council and later Boniface VIII (VI, 1, 6, 18) used their power of devolution to transfer the nomination from an incompetent chapter to the metropolitan or the pope. The electoral college sealed its own fate. In various ways and for diverse reasons the papacy took its place.

(*b*) The deficiencies of the electoral college had opened up the way to papal nominations. We have mentioned the frequency of the former. We now need to state more precisely what were the conditions of the latter.

In virtue of the *sollicitudo omnium ecclesiarum* according to which the Roman Pontiff was entrusted with the care of the whole Church, the pope was qualified to appoint a competent pastor in each diocese. The habit of intervening energetically in order to restore the dignity of the episcopate which the Gregorian papacy developed added the force of usage to the juridical principle. The papacy was already disposed to intervene but it was drawn in by the frequency of the appeals addressed to it.

The political importance of the episcopate was another reason for Rome to intervene. In the course of his conflict with Frederick II Innocent IV was anxious to secure for himself the services of devoted bishops and so made extensive use of the power of nomination. Similar political reasons explain nominations in Portugal, Scotland and Hungary. In order to fight against Albigensianism, Gregory IX and then Innocent IV demanded that the person elected by the chapter should be approved by their legates. St Louis protested against these Roman interventions in the name of the 'liberties of the Gallican Church'. These interventions infringed the electoral right which the title *De electione* of the Decretals of Gregory IX (I, 6) nevertheless consecrated. The practice was so irregular that Innocent IV himself on 23 May 1252 revoked all the direct nominations which had been extracted from him through 'improper requests'. But the abuses recurred, since Alexander IV in his turn revoked some of his predecessor's designations (Bull *Execrabilis quorumdam ambitio*). What had been more and more frequent practice received the sanction of law. In the name of the *plenitudo potestatis*, which the canonists of the thirteenth century magnified, the pope, 'whose will was reason' (Bernard of Parma), could dispose of bishoprics. Procedures were elaborated to reserve the filling of bishoprics to the Holy See in more and more cases. We cannot study these here in detail.

The 'providing mandates' which appeared in 1246 were issued in the name of *plenitudo potestatis*. In 1278 Nicholas III through his decretal *Cupientes* substituted the pope for the ordinary authorities (cathedral chapter or metropolitan) in case of disputed elections, transferences, resignations, suspensions, the dismissal of the holder of an office as well as devolution or reservation. This latter right had been instituted in 1265 by Clement IV and was then extended to more and more cases by Boniface VIII,

Clement V, John XXII (in the Constitution *ex debito*, 1316). In 1363 Urban V proclaimed his rights to designate patriarchs, archbishops, bishops, abbots and abbesses throughout Christendom. With rare exceptions, nomination had in fact taken the place of election.

Such right of nomination can be seen to be one further expresssion of the centralisation and absolutism of Rome which had continued to develop since Gregory VII. The authority of Rome was reinforced by the exploitation of old maxims recovered from Justinian's Digest and Code and it was served by the determination and prestige of a line of great pontiffs from Alexander III to John XXII. So the authority of Rome came to be felt everywhere and its interventions were facilitated and justified by the failings of local chapters.

Hierarchic centralisation and pastoral concern were, however, not the only determinants of the new policy. Other factors help to explain the attitude of the papacy; they might be contingent but they were pressing.

The right to dispose of bishoprics allowed many peoples' appetites to be satisfied. The size of the revenues and the prestige of the title attracted many candidates. The popes could in this way gratify their families and familiars in the way that the feudal chiefs had formerly been able to do.[3] And their own clientele was swollen by those of their entourage, and especially the cardinals who pressed the claims of their own dependents to the rich bishoprics. Princes too asked the pope to appoint their relatives, officers and counsellors to benefices.[4] The requirement of residence and therefore of the duties of bishops was interpreted widely, and this facilitated the disposal of bishoprics for personal ends.

Further, the requests were only one side of the coin, profits were the other. From the middle of the thirteenth century onwards, the bishop had to make a financial contribution to the pope over and above the expenses of the chancellery, on the occasion of his confirmation or nomination: not only the personal 'offerings' to the staff of the curia but above all the 'common offerings' shared by the Apostolic Camera and the Sacred College which amounted to a third of the annual revenues of benefices. On top of this the papacy added the 'annates', that is to say, the first year's revenues of benefices granted. This is what led Clement IV to say in 1267 that he 'blushed' at the sums raised from the dioceses in this way. Despite this scruple, the practice persisted. The financial needs of the Avignon papacy are well known. Nominations to bishoprics helped to satisfy them.

### 3. THE MAIN CONSEQUENCES

The variety of ways in which nominations came to take the place of elections, the diversity of local situations, the variability of pressure of demand upon the pope from his entourage, all go to explain why the change did not happen in one fell swoop, at a precise date and throughout Christendom.

We have already seen that election has persisted into our own time. But the two systems coexisted, especially for the last decades of the thirteenth century to the middle of the fourteenth century. The system of nomination, it is true, ceaselessly made progress, although it did sometimes yield to the electoral system. It has been reckoned that between 1227 and 1303 the pope made more than 1,400 nominations to bishoprics. In Bordeaux there were 3 between 1200 and 1247 and 21 between 1261 and 1314.[5]

What is more important than these reversals, which did not alter the general direction of change, are the effects of the new regime on the choice of bishops and on diocesan life.

When the bishop was chosen by the chapter, often enough among his own people, he would usually come from the diocese. Entrusted with its care, he remained faithful to it and the mystical marriage contracted on the occasion of his consecration hardly suffered any break. This is why he ruled so long, terminated only by the death of the prelate.

When the bishop came to be nominated, the story was different. Chosen by the pope, the bishop often belonged to the latter's circle or to that of those who had petitioned on his behalf. The diocese to which he became assigned was often unknown to him[6] and even if he resided there he was not very attached to it. After a few years he would move on to another see, either at the will of the Holy See or at his own wish. Transfers, which are in principle contrary to the mystical bond between the bishop and his church and which was for long regarded as exceptional and unseemly, became the norm. Family reasons, the attraction of a more agreeable residence, or of a more profitable benefice, the proximity of princes or kings, dictated these changes. The interest of the faithful was no longer the governing factor in the development of episcopal careers which converged on Rome . . . or Avignon.

This is the way in which a new episcopate to which emperors and kings paid attention took shape. It became the object of negotiations between princes and Rome. To restrict ourselves to the example of France, the Concordat of Bologna attests the importance attached to it by the 'very Christian king'.

*Translated by Iain McGonagle*


*Notes*

1. This is the reason why there is a different discipline in the Eastern Churches (Melchite, Maronite, Syrian, Chaldean, Coptic, Armenian) where the principle of election has survived better.

2. A French translation of most of the texts quoted here is to be found in *Les Elections dans l'Eglise latine des origines au XVIe siecle* eds. J. Gaudemet, J. Dubois, A. Duval, J. Champagne (Paris 1979).

3. Bertrand de Got who became Pope Clement V did not forget his family; Le Quercy, John XXII's country, and the Auvergne, where Urban V came from, supplied numerous bishops. The Avignon popes entrusted more than 45 bishoprics to their chaplains, chamberlains and treasurers.

4. In 1243 Innocent IV decided an electoral dispute in favour of Pierre Charlot, natural son of Philippe Auguste. In France, during the whole course of the fourteenth century chancellors, counsellors and members of parliament often benefited from papal nominations at the request of their masters.

5. Between 1317 and 1378 there were 4 nominations to 1 election in the province of Bordeaux, but 46 to 50 in that of Toulouse, 81 to 83 in that of Bourge. During the eighteen years of his pontificate John XXII made 780 nominations throughout christendom.

6. A canon of Orleans became archbishop of Aix in 1257. In the fourteenth century no bishop of Provence came from that region.

Bernhard Schimmelpfennig

# The Principle of the *Sanior Pars* in the Election of Bishops during the Middle Ages

IN 1215 the procedure for the election of bishops was established by the Fourth Lateran Council in its canon 24,[1] which soon afterwards was incorporated into the official canon law of the Church.[2] From now on only three forms of election were permitted: *per scrutinium, per compromissum, quasi per inspirationem*. The usual form was the first of these. In this three scrutineers (*scrutatores*) appointed by the cathedral chapter acting as an electoral college elicited and recorded the votes. Elected was the person who gained the support of everyone or of 'the larger and sounder parts of the chapter'.[3] This provision presupposed that by 1215 the electorate had at least in legal theory been narrowed down to the cathedral chapter and that more or less concrete ideas about the 'soundness' of particular electors were already in existence. Hence the first thing we need to tackle is the historical background to this conciliar decision.

The starting point for the development of the doctrine of the *sanior pars* is provided by the provision of the Rule of St Benedict for the election of the abbot: elected is the monk chosen by the entire community or by even a small part of it 'if its counsel be more wholesome' [*saniore consilio*].[4] How this soundness or wholesomeness is expressed is not specified by St Benedict. The final appeal and confirmation of this quality rested merely with God. This shows that St Benedict's provision was not a legal formula but a spiritual claim on the electors for the protection of possible minorities. A similar vagueness is to be found in most of the other formulations from the early Middle Ages. And as in the case of St Benedict they usually designated the electors' intentions rather than the electors themselves. When the electors were characterised, it was the elites of the clergy and laity (*maiores et meliores*, etc.), corresponding to the class structure of society. This structure was alluded to by an appeal on behalf of the candidate opposed to the eventual Pope Sergius III in 898. This appeal anticipated later formulations[5] even if weight of numbers was balanced not by soundness but by holiness.

The doctrine and subsequently the practice of ecclesiastical elections changed with the Church reforms in the eleventh century.[6] The reformers' aim was to exclude all non-clerical influence on the occupation of ecclesiastical offices in order to secure the 'freedom of the Church'—which to an increasingly strong extent was understood as a community predominantly determined by the clergy. To this end two measures needed above all to be adopted and implemented: the stress on actual election as opposed to other forms of installation in office (up till now election, acclamation and liturgical rites had been seen as actions of equal value), and the clear determination and gradual limitation of the body of electors. This design was of course not to be achieved all at once; and beyond this the intentions of the reformers of the eleventh century seem in part to have differed from those of the twelfth century, as is indicated by extant evidence. What was important for the supporters of Gregory VII was above all the positive intentions of the electors. Hence Gregory VII himself wrote of the 'better and more religious part of the people and clergy' or of the 'more devout and religious part', and at Augsburg in 1078 Wigold was elected by the 'better and larger part of those holding office in the Church'.[7] A more precise formulation was already provided by Ivo of Chartres in a letter to Paschal II about the election of the bishop of Beauvais when he wrote of the 'clergy with better reputations and healthier views'.[8] But even this formulation remained equivocal. Usually St Benedict's stipulation was simply transferred in a somewhat altered form to the election of bishops. And when this 'more wholesome counsel' was subjected to scrutiny, this was done not so much by ecclesiastical higher authorities as by secular rulers, as Calixtus II explicitly conceded to the German king in the Worms Concordat of 1122. It is not therefore surprising that even in the eleventh and twelfth centuries it was predominantly the secular rulers who decided in the case of disputed elections and that besides them and the local clergy it was the more powerful sections of the laity who determined the selection of candidates.[9] It was only rarely, as for example in the schismatic papal elections of 1130 and 1159, that the electors themselves claimed to be the 'larger and sounder part' (1130) or the 'sounder part' (1159). But frequently more important in episcopal elections was the amount a candidate paid to the supervising authority.

But from the 1130s onwards the way was prepared, at least in legal theory, for the limitation of the electorate to the cathedral chapter and an increased importance for the *sanior pars*. The conditions for this were the growing consolidation of the cathedral chapter as a corporation and the example of the college of cardinals as the exclusive electorate when it came to choosing a pope.[10] Already in 1139 the Second Lateran Council was forced to intervene against the exclusion of religious from episcopal elections; if the laity were mentioned then it was usually to reject their participation in the election of a bishop. Hence it is not surprising that from the middle of the twelfth century onwards—beginning in France particularly—cathedral chapters claimed the exclusive right of election for themselves and had this claim upheld by the popes. In a letter to the cathedral chapter of Arras, Alexander III underlined the importance of the 'larger and sounder part', which on the analogy of the Rule of St Benedict he interpreted as the 'part with the majority and sounder view'.[11] In 1179 the same pope saw to it that the Third Lateran Council decreed that in cases of dispute over the decisions of cathedral chapters the opinion of the 'larger and sounder part of the chapter' should prevail, unless the minority had well-founded objections to raise.[12] The cathedral chapter was thus given sanction as a corporation; in the case of decisions, among which elections were of course included, the burden of proof rested with the minority. In their coronation promises in 1209 and 1213 the future emperors Otto IV and Frederick II had to swear to uphold not just the freedom of ecclesiastical elections but the limitation of the electoral college to the cathedral chapter and the importance of the *maior et sanior pars*.[13] Politically the way was now prepared for the 1215 canon quoted at the start of this article.

The particular significance of the 1215 decree lay in the fact that from now on the principle of the *sanior pars* applied to ecclesiastical elections throughout the entire Church, whereas previously it had been of legal importance at the most in individual regions only. The one exception was the election of a new pope, for which a two-thirds majority had been needed since the Third Lateran Council in 1179, since there was no higher authority to examine and confirm the question of 'soundness'. The occasion for this reform had been the schismatic election of 1159 in which the minority party supporting Victor IV described itself as the *sanior pars*. But the 1215 decree had the not entirely welcome consequence that a spiritual criterion now had to be given a legal definition that would attract the least objections and that could be assessed as an argument in law-suits. The popes from Gregory IX onwards and contemporary and subsequent canonists took the trouble to do this. They sought to clarify who the *pars maior et sanior* might be, how they were to be recognised and who was competent to pronounce on 'soundness' in disputed elections.

An important role in the process of clarification was played by Gregory IX's decretal *In Genesi* which laid down how what was termed the *collatio*, the business of comparing and weighing the votes cast by the various electors, was to be conducted.[14] In disputed elections the number of votes, the zeal and the merit of the various factions had to be compared and assessed. In another decretal dealing with a double election in Châlons-sur-Marne this same pope decided that the election was invalid because the majority was not the *pars sanior*: the minority could lay claim to greater merit and authority.[15]

It was above all on the basis of these two decretals that the canonists of the thirteenth century made clear who was to be described as *pars sanior*. For this it was necessary to define the concepts of zeal (*zelus*), merit (*meritum*), and authority (*auctoritas*). But it was only to a limited extent that they were able to work out a unanimous view. Reference to the most important commentaries will help to illustrate the various different standpoints. In his commentary, which received wide circulation as the *Glossa ordinaria*, Bernard de Botone demanded of electors and candidates *zelus*, and in addition of candidates *merita* and of electors *dignitas*, so that on the basis of all these factors the larger and sounder part could be recognised.[16] Elsewhere he identified *auctoritas* with the dignities held by members of the chapter and with merits achieved in the course of life, *zelus* with the intention of voting without regard for human considerations; in keeping with this he described that party as *maior et sanior* that was motivated by greater zeal and greater piety.[17]

A more differentiated judgment and one that to some extent diverges from this was reached by Godfrey of Trani in his much-admired *Summa*.[18] He provided predominantly negative definitions for the concepts *zelus* and *meritum*: someone who was under the penalty of major excommunication, suspension or interdict, who voted for someone who was unworthy or who did not observe the electoral procedure—such a person did not possess *zelus*; whereas insufficient *merita* were displayed by someone who was of illegitimate birth or was not to be recommended on account of his way of life and knowledge, who was younger than thirty years of age or was under the penalty of excommunication, suspension or interdict. The former ought not to vote, the latter ought not to be elected. He drew the conclusion: 'To be elected is the person who appears worthier, for the party that nominates the worthier candidate displays the better *zelus*. Hence it is to be regarded as the sounder even if it does not enjoy a majority, since *zelus* is made up of two factors, the authority of the electors and the worth of the person elected.'[19] But to be elected a person had to have the support both of an absolute majority and of the *pars sanior*.

The criteria developed by Godfrey were taken over and expanded by Henry of Susa, known as Hostiensis from his being cardinal bishop of Ostia. *Sanior* he identified with *zelus*, 'which is made up of three components: the suitability of the person elected and the authority and spiritual intention of the electors'. But he placed the highest value on the candidate's suitability or qualifications, since those who voted for the candidate who displayed the greatest merits should themselves too possess the better *zelus*.[20] In contrast to Godfrey and showing a greater realism he explained who it was who lacked *zelus*: the person who was motivated by entreaties, money or fear.[21]

Innocent IV on the other hand used positive terminology to define *zelus* in his commentary. It consisted of greater authority, greater dignity, higher orders, greater age and greater piety. More simply and more clearly than Hostiensis, he made *merita* refer to the person elected and *zelus* to the electors.[22]

The canonists were thus agreed only on the need, in keeping with Gregory IX's decretals, to investigate *meritum* and *zelus* in the case of disputed elections. But whether the *pars sanior* ascertained by this investigation was by preference to be identified with the majority was asserted by some and denied by others. Equally disputed were the criteria whereby *zelus* and *meritum*—and thus the *pars sanior*—were to be precisely ascertained. No wonder that in many double elections all the parties claimed to be the *pars sanior*. Investigation and decision rested with the *superior* to whom they appealed, and with ever-increasing frequency this was the pope. Hence the principle of the *senior pars* in fact contributed to the papacy intervening ever more decisively in the election of bishops and reserving to itself the filling of episcopal sees. In other cases, as in England and France, the secular rulers took advantage of prevailing conditions and despite ecclesiastical regulations to the contrary continued the policies of their predecessors in earlier centuries.

A further disadvantage of the electoral procedure of the time was the limitation of the electorate to the cathedral chapter. The election of a bishop was in fact used by many cathedral chapters to wrest some measure of influence over the way the bishopric was run, through electoral capitulations and the selection of suitably biddable candidates. Where this did not happen cathedral chapters often developed into a counter-administration in opposition to the bishop. To this was added the personal composition of the chapter. Usually its members represented the leading elites of the region at the time. No wonder that the selection of candidates for the bishopric was used to safeguard the interests of these classes of society. Hence disputed elections often reflected conflicts between different regional power-blocs. This tendency was strengthened still more in countries where with the help of the papacy the central power had been weakened or completely eliminated, as in Germany or northern Italy. Hence in Germany elections, when possible, served to stabilise territorial domination and in northern Italy communal regimes or newly emerging *signorie*. It is clear that the papacy too made use of episcopal elections to build up the states of the Church in central Italy. Investigation of *zelus* and *merita* was in consequence often merely the instrument provided by canon law to safeguard the dominant interests of the time, and the *maior et sanior pars* was thus the regional power-bloc that was strongest at that moment. Pressure, money and a skilful use of the papal power of dispensation could be applied further to 'improve' *zelus* and *merita*. No wonder that Innocent IV alone gave permission for 24 men of illegitimate birth—including 6 priests' sons and 1 bishop's son—to be ordained bishops, even though like all other canonists he had stressed in his commentary that illegitimate birth was an impediment to election as a bishop.[23]

The upshot was that efforts began to be made to abandon the principle of the *sanior pars* in favour of the unconditional principle of the majority.[24] The Bolognese canonist Tancred had already stressed the *maior pars*. Innocent IV wrote that 'the truth is better recognised by means of a majority'. To this was added the concern of popes from Alexander IV onwards not to become involved in every quarrel over episcopal elections. Hence the Second Council of Lyons decided under the leadership of Gregory X in 1274 that, following the example of papal elections, the majority alone should be regarded as decisive when two-thirds of the electors were agreed in supporting one of the candidates. In such a case it would not be permitted to dispute the election on the basis of the criteria of *zelus*, *meritum* or *auctoritas*. The defeated minority had merely the opportunity of having the election declared null on the basis of the unsuitability of the candidate of the majority; but in this case the burden of proof rested with the minority. Johannes Andreae was thus right to deduce in his *Glossa ordinaria* on this decree 'Where the majority is, the presumption is that it is also the sounder part.'[25] And to make appeals to the apostolic see still more difficult Gregory X, Nicholas III and Boniface VIII proclaimed sanctions against appellants who disputed majority elections on trifling grounds or with unfounded accusations. Similarly material pressure was forbidden at episcopal elections.[26] But this did not mean that a majority sufficed at every election of a bishop. When a two-thirds majority was lacking the minority could continue to describe itself as *sanior pars* and dispute the election. And despite the limitation of the electorate to the cathedral chapter the possibility of opposition existed for those who were not electors and indeed even for the laity, as Johannes Andreae emphasised.[27] Grounds for disputing the election that were satisfactory from the point of view of canon law were of course necessary. And because the same canonist drew attention to the fact that not everybody had a sufficient knowledge of the procedure to be followed in elections *per scrutinium*[28] it can be presumed that procedural mistakes provided a welcome opportunity to dispute episcopal elections.

The procedure followed or not followed at elections did not in any case stop the majority principle establishing itself ever more strongly at the expense of the *sanior pars*. The popes of the later thirteenth century, such as Nicholas IV, were already often emphasising in their writings merely the majority—that is, when they had not already reserved the filling of the see concerned to themselves. And when councils, such as those of Constance and Basle, dealt with episcopal elections they mentioned only the majority and no longer the *sanior pars*. Hence the latter no longer had any part to play at all at the Council of Trent with all its important consequences.[29]

The principle of the *sanior pars* did, however, remain in existence. Its survival was above all due to the academic bias shown by the canonists' activity. Without regard for the conciliar decree of 1274 they followed their predecessors in commenting on the decretals of Innocent III and Gregory IX. Typical was Guillaume de Mandagout, whose treatise on elections achieved the greatest success. Like Innocent IV he regarded *zelus* as the criterion by which the electors should be judged, while *merita* served for the recognition of the worthier candidate. And he followed Hostiensis in describing the positive and negative characteristics of *zelus* and *meritum*. What, however, raised his treatise above the level of most other treatments of elections were his suggested formulae for publicising elections and for documents in law-suits, since in these the otherwise mainly theoretical exposition of *zelus*, *meritum* and *sanior pars* is developed as an aid in argumentation.[30]

But even among the canonists the preference for the majority established itself even more strongly. Thus Johannes Andreae, the most influential canonist of the later Middle Ages, emphasised that a minority was to be regarded as *sanior pars* and as a consequence the candidate of the majority was not elected only if the *auctoritas* and *meritum* of the minority far exceeded those of the majority and if there was only a small difference in the number of votes cast for each candidate.[31] But usually it was assumed that the majority also displayed proper and adequate *zelus*. If, however, the electors *zelus* needed investigation, then this was done with reference above all to negative characteristics such as human greed, showing preference to relatives, old age and infirmity, lack of qualifications, or hatred for the candidate one was not supporting.[32] John of Anagni even outdid this definition by providing only a negative description of *zelus*.[33] Hence it was only *meritum* that could still be given a positive interpretation. It is thus not surprising that round about 1400 Antonio da Butrio replaced *meritum* by *sanioritas* and went on to elucidate this concept in another passage: 'The *sanioritas* of the electors is for the most part discerned from the character of the person elected.'[34] What was important for fifteenth-century canon law and for that of early modern times was that Nicholas de Tudeschis, known as Panormitanus through his having been archbishop of Palermo, clung to this narrowing down in a somewhat attenuated formulation, even if he was also concerned to work the classical teaching of the thirteenth century into his commentary.[35]

Usually statements of this kind remained without practical significance, since the filling of episcopal sees had become a privilege of the papacy or of the secular ruler. But when a power vacuum existed, as in seventeenth-century Germany, the old teaching awoke to a new life and even the principle of the *sanior pars* could then, as centuries earlier, serve different factions of voters as an argument in their efforts to make their interests prevail.[36] But the usefulness of this principle from the point of view of canon law—leaving spiritual intentions completely on one side—was just as slight at this time as during the Middle Ages.

*Translated by Robert Nowell*

*Notes*

1. *Conciliorum Oecumenicorum* (Bologna ³1973) p. 246.

2. X 1.6.42. To save space, papal decretals are cited according to the now usual convention: collection (X = *Decretales Gregorii IX*, VI = *Liber Sextus*), book, title, chapter. They have been edited by E. Friedburg *Corpus iuris canonici* (Leipzig 1881, reprinted Graz 1959) II.

3. The council's wording is *maior vel sanior pars capituli*, the decretal's *maior et sanior pars capituli*.

4. *Benedicti regula* ed. R. Hanslik (CSEL 75) (Vienna 1960) p. 148, ch. 64 § 1: *pars quamvis parva congregationis saniore consilio*; *The Rule of St Benedict*, translated and edited by Abbot Justin McCann, O.S.B. (London ²1960) p. 145. For developments in the early middle ages, see E. Ruffini Avondo 'Il Principio maggioritario nella storia del Diritto Canonico', in *Archivio Giuridico 'Filippo Serafini'* 4 ser. 9 (1925) 15-67; A. Carboni ' *"Sanior pars" ed elezioni episcopali fino alla lotta per le investiture*' op. cit. 6 ser. 27 (1960) 76-127; A. Carboni *'L'influenza della Regula S. Benedicti sul regime delle elezioni episcopali'* op. cit. 6 ser. 28 (1960) 34-38; H. Grundmann *'Pars quamvis parva. Zur Abtswahl nach Benedikts Regel'* in *Festschrift P.E. Schramm* (Wiesbaden 1964) I. pp. 237-251.

5. Auxilius against Sergius III: *maior et sanctior* (sic.) *cleri et populi pars*, cited by E. Ruffini Avondo in the article cited in note 4 at p. 110.

6. In addition to the literature cited in note 4, see P. Schmid *Der Begriff der kanonischen Wahl in den Anfängen des Investiturstreits* (Stuttgart 1926); P. Hofmeister ' "Pars sanioris consilii" (Regula c. 64)', in *Studien und Mitteilungen zur Geschichte des Benediktinerordens* 70 (1959-60) 12-24.

7. Gregory VII: *pars cleri et populi melior et religiosior*, quoted by P. Hofmeister, in the article cited in note 6 at p. 13; Augsburg: *a meliori et amriori parte ecclesiasticae militiae*, quoted by A. Cargoni, in article cited in note 4 at p. 122.

8. P. Hofmeister, in the article cited in note 6 at p. 14: *clerici melioris famae et consilii sanioris*.

9. J. Bauermann *'Die Frage der Bischofswahlen auf dem Würzburger Reichstag von 1133'* in *Festschrift Robert Holtzmann* (Berlin 1933) pp. 103-134; F. Geselbracht *Das Verfahren bei den deutschen Bischofswahlen in der zweiten Hälfte des 12. Jahrhunderts* (Phil. Diss. Leipzig) (Weida 1905); M. Pacaut *Louis VII et les élections épiscopales dans le royaume de France 1137-1180* (Paris 1957); R. H. Schmandt 'The Election and Assassination of Albert of Louvain, Bishop of Liège, 1191-92' in *Speculum* 42 (1967) 639-660.

10. K. Ganzer 'Zur Beschränkung der Bischofswahl auf die Domkapitel in Theorie und Praxis des 12. und 13. Jahrhunderts', in *Zeitschrift für Rechtsgeschichte, Kanonische Abteilung* 57 (1971) 22-82, and 58 (1972) 166-197.

11. J. Ramackers *Papsturkunden in Frankreich N.F. 3, Artois* (Göttingen 1940) pp. 169-170, no. 108 (undated, circa 1159-81): *maior et sanior pars* and *pars fratrum maioris et sanioris consilii*.

12. Canon 16: *Conciliorum Oecumenicorum Decreta* pp. 219-220, X 3.11.1.

13. *Monumental Germaniae Historica, Constitutiones* II p. 37 no. 31 § 2 and p. 58, no. 46f. § 2.

14. X 1.6.55: *collatio numeri ad numerum, zeli ad zelum, meriti ad meritum*.

15. X 1.6.57 '*Ecclesia vestra*'. The majority argued: *maiorem capituli partem habetat, et per hoc debebat pars sua sanior reputari, cum, ubi maior numerus est, zelus melior presumatur*. The minority argued: *electores cardinalis* (i.e., the minority) *alios meritis et auctoritate precellerent, habito presertim respectu ad personam electam, meliorem zelum eos habuisse constabat*.

16. *Glossa ordinaria* on X 1.6.55, v. '*Ad zelum*'.

17. *Glossa ordinaria* on X 1.6.57, v. '*Non consenserit*'.

18. Gottofredo da Trani *Summa super titulis decretalium* (Lyons 1519, reprinted Aalen 1968) 10vb-15vb.

19. *Ibid.* 12va: *Eligendus est is, qui dignior esse videtur; nam pars illa, que in scrutinio nominat digniorem, in meliori zelo consistit; propterea, si non maior numero, sanior tamen esse censetur, quia zelus consideratur ex duobus, scilicet ex auctoritate eligentium et dignitate electi*.

20. Henricus de Segusio (Hostiensis) *In V decretalium libros commentaria* (Venice 1581, reprinted Turin 1965) I 77vb on X 1.6.55, v. '*Sanior*' and '*Nec plene*'. See also *op. cit.* 79vb on X 1.6.57, v. '*Meritis*', '*Et auctoritate*' and '*Zelum*'.

21. Henricus de Segusio *Summa* (Lyons 1537, reprinted Aalen 1962) 19vb *De electione* no. 12.

22. K. Ganzer *Papsttum und Bischofsbesetzungen in der Zeit von Gregor IX. bis Bonifaz VIII.* (Cologne/Graz 1968) pp. 12-18.

23. B. Schimmelpfennig 'Zölibat und Lage der "Priestersöhne" vom 11. bis 14. Jahrhundert' in *Historische Zeitschrift* 227 (1978) 38. On the practice of elections in the thirteenth century, see K. Ganzer *Papsttum* (note 22 above), passim; G. Barraclough 'The Making of a Bishop in the Middle Ages' in *The Catholic Historical Review* 19 (1933-34) 275-319; E. Roland *Les Chanoines et les élections épiscopales du XI<sup>e</sup> au XIV<sup>e</sup> siècle* (Aurillac 1909) pp. 73-228; K. Ganzer '*Zur Beschränkung . . .*' second article (note 10 above).

24. K. Ganzer '*Zur Beschränkung . . .*' first article (note 10 above) 77-78; O. von Gierke *Das deutsche Genossenschaftsrecht* (reprinted Darmstadt 1954) III pp. 322 ff.; A. Esmein 'L'unanimité et la majorité dans les élections canoniques', in *Mélanges Fitting* (Montpellier 1907), reprinted Aalen/Frankfurt, 1979) I pp. 355-382, especially pp. 379-380. Innocent IV's comment on X 1.6.42 (Gierke p. 324): *quia per plures melius veritas inquiritur*.

25. VI 1.6.9 '*Si quando*'. *Glossa ordinaria*, before the *Casus: tamen, ubi est maior pars, presumitur, quod etiam sit sanior*.

26. VI 1.6.11, 12, 16, 29.

27. *Glossa ordinaria* on VI 1.6.16, v. '*Unicus*'.

28. *Glossa ordinaria* on VI 1.6.29, v. '*Inquisitis*'.

29. Conc. Const. sess. XV c. 26; Conc. Basil. sess. XII *de electionibus*; Conc. Trid. sess. VI c. 1 *de residentia*, VII c. 1 *de reformatione*, XXII c. 2 *de reformatione*, XXIV c. 1 *de reformatione* (*Conciliorum Oecumenicorum Decreta* pp. 431, 469-472, 681-682, 687, 738, 759-761.

30. Guillelmus Mandagotus *Tractatus de electionibus novorum praelatorum* (Cologne 1574) 44v, 58v-61v, 125v-134v, 151v-169r: ch. 22, 31, 59, 60.

31. Johannes Andreae *In I decretalium novella commentaria* (Venice 1581, reprinted Turin 1963) 133vb on the final *Glossa ordinaria* on X 1.6.57.

32. *Ibid.* 133va on the final *Glossa ordinaria* on X 1.6.57, v. '*Auctoritas*'.

33. Johannes Monachus *Glossa aurea super Sexto decretalium* (Paris 1535, reprinted Aalen 1968) 73va: Probus' supplement to VI 1.6.9, v. '*Zelus*'.

34. Antonius a Butrio *Super Prima Primi Decretalium Commentarii* (Venice 1578, reprinted Turin 1967) 137vb on X 1.6.42; 150ra on X 1.6.57: *Nota primo, quod principaliter ex persona electi colligitur sanioritas eligentium.*

35. E. Ruffini Avondo in the article cited in note 4 at pp. 60-61, 63; A. Esmein in the article cited in note 24 at pp. 375-376.

36. H. E. Feine *Die Besetzung der Reichsbistümer vom Westfälischen Frieden bis zur Säkularisation 1648-1803* (Stuttgart 1905, reprinted Amsterdam 1964) pp. 207-211.

Jean Bernhard

# The Election of Bishops at the Council of Trent

SINCE the election of bishops by the community had already been overtaken by their nomination *de facto* by the pope in the thirteenth and fourteenth centuries the subject of this article may appear rather surprising. Before that time the role of the laity (with the exception of some rulers) and of a large part of the clergy in such elections had been gradually eliminated.[1]

In law, however, the nomination of bishops was not reserved to the Holy See until the 1917 Code of Canon Law.[2] The few elections which still exist today[3] are exceptions to which the papacy has given its consent.

In so far as the Council of Trent is concerned, can. 8 of the decree on the sacrament of Order (XXIIIrd Session) simply states: 'Whoever says that bishops appointed (*assumuntur*) by the authority of the Roman Pontiff are neither true not legitimate bishops but a human invention, let him be anathema.' And the first canon of the Reform Decree (Session XXIV) only lays down certain rules to be observed for the nomination of bishops: 'The Council ordains that as soon as a church falls vacant the chapter will order public and private prayers and supplications in order that God may grant clergy and people a good pastor.' Any investigation about the candidate's aptitude must be sent to Rome where it will be studied by the cardinal in charge of the report with three other cardinals; this report of the cardinals will be read out in consistory, while the final judgment is left to another consistory. This will enable the pope to provide the church in question with the right bishop as he will be fully cognisant of the case and the persons involved.[4]

These texts of the Council of Trent are well known. What is less well known is how the conciliar Fathers came to approve them.

In fact a lively debate showed up a major split between the bishops. It occupied the Council from 12 May till 16 June 1563. On the one hand, the minority, mainly composed of the French and Spanish bishops, insisted on a return to the practice of the early Church for the choice of bishops. On the other hand, the majority view, heavily backed by the Italian *zelanti*, was that the *status quo* should be maintained with slight alterations. The purpose of this article is to provide a methical overview of this episode in the Council. It is, however, too limited in space to deal with all the aspects involved, even briefly.

First of all, the debate about the election of bishops has to be put in its historical and theological context. In February 1563 the Council was in a state of crisis. The decrees on the sacrament of Order and the residence of bishops remained in suspense. The critical issue was whether bishops held their jurisdiction directly from God through their episcopal ordination (the episcopalian line) or from the pope (the presbyterial line, which saw the difference between bishop and priest mainly as a jurisdictional matter). At the Council the two opposing views were locked in a powerful confrontation.

The two opposing sides also confronted each other from another and more concrete point of view. The Italian *zelanti*, re-grouped under the leadership of the Cardinal Legate Simonetta, were bent on stressing the primacy of the pope and consequently wanted to maintain the function of the curia as it existed. On the other hand, the 'episcopalians' were vitally concerned with bringing about a reform of the Church in depth and by implication wanted to strengthen the authority of the bishops.

In the background of all this there loomed a sharp awareness of the vital thesis of the Reformation which reduced the function of the ministry to serving the Word of God while on the Catholic side there was a remarkable lack of any genuine 'theology of the Word'.

With these main lines of the confrontation in mind we can now pursue the principal points of the debate as it developed.[5]

On 13 February 1563 a conciliar commission was set up charged with a project which would deal with *Canones super abusibus circa administrationem sacramenti ordinis*. The leading role here was played by the archbishop of Sens and the bishop of Verdun, particularly with regard to the canon which concerned the qualities which a candidate for the episcopacy should have. In actual fact, the text does not specify which body should choose the candidate but it accepts that the clergy and the people have a part to play in the nomination procedure. At the request of the archbishop, the chapter of the vacant church posts the candidate's name and Christian name for fifteen days. Both clergy and people are told that if anyone has an objection to a candidate he is completely free to make his objection plain to the archbishop or bishops (*ut omnes, si quid habent adversus ipsum promovendum, ipso archiepiscopo seu episcopis libere patefaciant*). On some given day the members of the chapter and the representatives of the secular and regular diocesan clergy meet with the archbishop and at least two bishops of the province in question. Then the candidate himself presents the testimonies in favour of his nomination! After the sermon he would have to preach in the presence of the clergy or 'in public', there was again an opportunity to express objections to his nomination. When the archbishop and bishops had discussed all this with the members of the chapter, they would pass on to Rome their own opinion of the candidate as well as the official record of the whole investigation. The whole of this report would then be read out at the consistory. And so the pope should be able to proceed to the nomination with a clearer understanding of the case.

Most of the Conciliar Fathers were obviously keen on filling the vacant sees with the best possible candidates. Yet, canon 1 of the project also brought out, at least partially, the 'policy' of the French bishops: to give the clergy and the people a say in the appointment of their bishop. The document was handed to the cardinal legates on 1 April, and was, without alterations, transmitted to the bishops and ambassadors on 29 April, in spite of the pope's reservations. He was worried about the way in which this process hampered his freedom to nominate bishops. The suppression of canon 1 was also demanded by two ambassadors who maintained that it undermined their sovereign's right to such a nomination. The cardinal legates strongly objected to this because, in their view, legates to the Council were not entitled to change a text worked out by the conciliar commission nor to impose any modification on this commission. The freedom of the Council had to be protected at all costs.

Discussion of the project was initiated at the General Assembly of 12 May. The

Cardinal of Lorraine, still the leader of the 'episcopalian' opposition, rejected canon 1 as too 'conservative'. In a brilliant speech he insisted that the primitive community had the right to choose its own bishop as demonstrated by numerous quotations from the New Testament (*quid Christus ordinaverit et quid in primitiva Ecclesia observatum fuerit*). He also quoted Cyprian's 67th letter in which he stressed the importance of the contribution by the people: the choice is willed by God because the people only interpret the will of God. And so, the Cardinal went on, nothing of what Cyprian reported and what was rooted in the apostolic tradition was any longer observed: now one was appointed archbishop without consulting the suffragan bishops, and bishop without consulting the metropolitan.

Next, the cardinal attacked the right to nominate claimed by the chapters and the temporal rulers. One could, if necessary, accept the latter if the ruler holds it *industria personae*, but what about this right if it is in the hands of young boys or even women *quae prohibentur in ecclesia loqui*? Finally the cardinal advised the pope to abandon his claim to the personal nomination of bishops if only to relieve his conscience.

The proposals contained in canon 1 and especially those launched by the Cardinal of Lorraine were fiercely criticised. There was a sharpening of the differences between the French 'episcopalians' and the Spanish ones. The Italian bishops, on the whole, were against the project which they thought too bold altogether. The core of the debate developed as follows.

Already on 13 May those on the side of the curia asked that canon 1 be suppressed 'because instead of eliminating abuses, it invited them'. The Archbishop of Otranto expressed his horror at the chaos that would result from the suggested procedure. How could one ask a candidate to prove that he was fit to be a bishop? And would the Kings of Spain and Portugal not object that their established rights would be violated? Cardinal Madruzzo thought that the project dealt with questions of detail although these could be more effectively dealt with by the provincial councils when required.

Other Italian bishops thought that canon 1 was unrealistic, superfluous (since the issue had already been disposed of by the Council in its XXIInd Session), and likely to lead to 'evils and scandals'. The Bishop of Parma was indeed a member of the commission which had drafted the project but made his opposition to the text perfectly clear. His colleague, the Bishop of Nicastro, admitted that he participated in the commission's draft of the project but asserted that the best way of appointing a bishop was to leave it to the pope.

The *votum* of the Archbishop of Rossano is worth looking at. He maintained that, when there are abuses because a law is not observed, people immediately jump to the idea that the solution is a new law; but it would be so much better to strengthen the law by laying down sanctions for its non-application. And he added that it was extremely difficult to work out a new general law: 'When a law is not adapted to the various local circumstances, it is quite possible that local practice does not back it up or that it is simply abrogated by being ignored.' So, how could the reform project be applied in Spain and Portugal without doing damage to the situation? Moreover, how can one expect a candidate to 'sing his own praises and lauding his own behaviour'? Anybody accepting this procedure would prove by the same token that he is totally unfit for the job.

In so far as participation by the people is concerned, the good Archbishop opined that 'the people are hopelessly superficial and it can be taken for granted that they are more moved by rhetoric, kindness, favours, serious requests and sometimes by bribes than by a straightforward sense of responsibility (*prudentia*)'. Moreover, since the people's faith seems to be wavering from one extreme to the other, would their participation not lead to a bishop in their own image? In the early Church the people came in *post factum*, when they gave their agreement to an appointment already made.

Where the people chose the candidate, the situation had changed. He did not want to go back in his days to a situation which scholars interpreted as usurpation.

The Spanish approach to the reform project was less 'revolutionary' than the French one, but no less radical for all that. On several points the Archbishops of Braga and Granada brought up the relevance of the situation in the early Church.

In the matter of episcopal appointments the Archbishop of Granada maintained that the reform could concentrate on the pastoral task which the bishop received directly from God. It was therefore important to appoint only those men who were best fitted to exercise this function. To achieve this several procedures were already available but none of them was infallible. The Archbishop thought that it was not necessary to deprive the King of Spain of his right to nominate bishops, but such a nomination should be preceded by a 'rigorous examination'. The Bishop of Segovia went into greater detail: there was no need to copy the practice of the early Church because there were several procedures even in those days. It was rather a matter of combining what was best. He himself was in favour of bringing the bishops and the archbishop of the province into the nominating procedure, but not the people ('one wonders whether somethings the *vox populi* is not the *vox* of the devil himself'). In any case, should one not query the mere papal confirmation of an appointment which is already a *fait accompli*?

The Bishop of Fünfkirchen had indeed close ties with the Cardinal of Lorraine as the official 'orator' of the emperor, but nevertheless could not agree with the cardinal's proposals. How could one possibly let the people participate in the matter of episcopal appointments when so many regions show that the people were losing their faith more and more? There was no doubt that the three ways of appointing a bishop existing at that time should be changed, and they could be changed.

According to this bishop, the cathedral chapters in Germany were entitled to elect the diocesan bishop. So, let the Council enforce the election of a member of this chapter and let it be seen to that there were members of the chapter who had the required qualities. Where the kings were concerned who had the right to nominate, they should not be allowed to exercise this right without consulting the bishops of the province concerned. The pope himself should, before canonically installing a candidate, whether elected or nominated, see to it that he was informed about the candidate's qualities through evidence gathered on the spot. And the curia should not limit itself to making sure that the candidate was able to pay his nomination fee.

The French bishops ranged themselves unanimously behind the Cardinal of Lorraine. The Bishop of Verdun even tried to tone down the differences between the French (Gallican) and the Spanish reform proposals. To put it briefly, they wanted to throw out canon 1 of the reform project as it had hardly anything new to offer. At the end of the debate Claude de Sainctes brought up once again the need to cut out the right of temporal rulers to nominate bishops. How could bishops protect their Church against royal intrusions when they were themselves appointed by the king? There was a chance here of doing away with the abuses which followed when a bishop was nominated by a woman or a young boy, so why not seize it?

And so we reach the last day of these General Assemblies (16 June 1563). Lainez, the Jesuit Superior General, started the debate all over again. He began by saying that man's inner conversion was the fruit of grace, and all that the reforming laws could do was to encourage this process. But to go back to the laws of the early Church where the appointment of bishops was concerned was a policy coming from the devil himself: those laws were not just 'ancient', they were 'antiquated'. Laws must yield to the law of charity (the only laws to be changed were those that went against charity). Now there were two ways of appointing bishops: this was done either by the clergy or by the laity. All these procedures were open to corruption, whether because of sin or because of errors besetting those who played a part in them. There was a hierarchy in elections involving human beings, and in this hierarchy an election by the clergy is superior to one conducted by the laity. Among the 'elections' conducted among the clergy the most 'worthy' is an election conducted by the pope, then one by the archbishop and bishops of a province, and finally one effectuated by the cathedral chapter. . . .

At this point the speaker brought in a qualification: the best procedure in theory is not necessarily the best practicable *hic et nunc*, where circumstances of time and place count. And, in any case, Lainez added, it was an error to assert that the bishops of the province had the power to elect by divine right, because, if it were so 'the bishops would not be bishops and the Church would be in error'.

At the end of the debate it was clear that a large majority of the Council Fathers rejected the French reform project. The Cardinal of Lorraine came out of the battle with his authority diminished as leader of the 'episcopalian' opposition. He also lost status with the French authorities because of the line he had taken with regard to the French King's right to appoint.

While the debate was still in progress there occurred two events which deserve to be mentioned.

On 2 June President de Birague, special envoy of Charles IX of France, brought out an alarming report on the religious situation in France: he had a letter from the King which he read out to the bishops. In it the King tried to justify the Peace of Amboise. And de Birague concluded that the only possible way of remedying the French situation lay in a profound reform of the Church brought about by the Council, not in a military victory over the Huguenots.

The other important event was the diplomatic success which Cardinal Morone had recently obtained at Innsbruck in his talks with the emperor. Morone was the new president of the college of legates to the Council. He managed to persuade the emperor that the pope was sincere when he said that he would not interrupt the Council. The emperor had always wanted the reform of the Church by the Council but without the Council tackling the thorny issue of the relationship between the papal primacy and the bishops.

The most difficult part of Morone's task still had to be done, namely the approval of the decree on the sacrament of order and the reform decree. Morone tried to have the decree on the sacrament of order amended in smaller and informal meetings. Several compromises were rejected either by one group or an other. The Cardinal of Lorraine and the French bishops continued to labour for a strong episcopacy, centred on solid powers of the metropolitan (those imbued with a kind of uncompromising Gallicanism would not let any expression which excluded the superiority of the General Council over the pope get into the formulation of the decree). The Spanish 'episcopalians' did not question the primacy of the pope but insisted that 'the episcopacy was instituted by Christ'. As to the Italian bishops, most of them were prepared to follow the conciliar policy pursued by the cardinal legates. The *zelanti*, however, rejected any formula which diverged from that of the Council of Florence where the primacy was concerned and any trend towards reforming the Church which they thought too radical. As the lobbying between the various groups proceeded, the Cardinal of Lorraine showed himself increasingly resigned to moderation. What had happened?

Did some kind of religious motivation lead him to some inner conversion? Was he shaken by President de Birague's report to the Council? Had he been influenced by the new conciliar policy followed by the emperor? Or had he perhaps pinned his hopes on a promise made to him in June that he would be promoted to pontifical legate if only he cooperated with the secret plan of the 'Pratica' (this plan was to wind up the Council as soon as possible and then to get on with the reform of the Church, country by country, presided over by a pontifical legate)? Perhaps all these motives played a part in the cardinal's sudden change of course.

Whatever the truth may be, on 23 June Pius IV demanded that Cardinal Morone should be officially informed of the secret plan of the 'Pratica'. The plan had been the brainchild of the Bishop of Viterbo, *ex-nuncio* to France. However, Morone refused to lend himself to this kind of political-religious combination. His only concern was to restore the Council to the proper pursuit of its task. On 19 June he sent to Rome a fresh recipe worked out in the talks on the decree of the Sacrament of Order. But he added the following warning: If the pope refused this formula G, the Council would be forced to tackle the ecclesiological problem in all its dimensions. In order to avoid that kind of risk Morone also suggested in the name of the college of legates the following procedure: the Council should limit itself to a short decree on the Sacrament of Order, leaving out any reference to the bishops' jurisdictional status (which means any reference to the institution of the episcopacy) and to the issue of papal primacy versus episcopacy.

On 9 July the pope's reply reached Trent. It showed that he was still unaware of the gravity of the situation within the Council. He just did not seem to realise the ecclesiological importance of the differences of opinion. He rejected formula G on the decree in question. He told Morone: 'Make sure of the consensus required to establish a dogma; in any case the proposed formula is far from clear.' What the pope was after was a downright statement that, first of all, bishops got their jurisdiction from the pope, and secondly that the Council re-affirm the formula of Florence in so far as the papal primacy was concerned.

In the meantime the pope had heard that formula G might not be agreed to at the Council. So he instructed Morone to limit his policy strictly to a decree on the Sacrament of Order, cutting out any reference to where the jurisdiction of the bishops came from.

Both papal messages arrived at Trent at the same time. As it happened, Cardinal Morone and the Cardinal of Lorraine had already reached the great decision which was supposed to 'save' the Council three days before.

On 6 July the influential members of the Council (Cardinals Guise and Madruzzo and some forty bishops of various nationalities) approved the brief formula of the decree on the Sacrament of Order as well as the decree on whether bishops should be resident.

On 9 July the formula was submitted to the General Assembly. The Spanish bishops expressed some doubts. They found that c. 6 which mentioned a *hierarchia divina ordinatione instituta* was much too vague and that this was moreover narrowed down by canon 8 which had not even been mentioned at a meeting of the influential members of the Council. All the same, the text was approved by a significant majority.

On the eve of the Session the Spanish section (about thirty bishops who supported the line of the Archbishop of Granada) once again declared their objection to c. 6, while the Italian *zelanti* thought that by making the obligatory residence of the bishop a matter of 'divine command', this decree on episcopal residence implied that this residential obligation was also of 'divine right'. But the cardinal legates refused to budge. They accepted the situation after an orally given promise of the legates to discuss the institution of bishops again later. The *zelanti*, afraid of undoing all the work Morone had put into achieving some kind of agreement, no longer insisted on their objection either.

The last days before the Session were also devoted to the actual formulation of the reform decree. Canon 1, which we have dealt with at length, was thoroughly re-modelled. The public 'examination' of the candidate was replaced by testimonials composed by the archbishop or two suffragan bishops of the province concerned and then looked into by four cardinals.

The debate on the new project was opened at the General Assembly of 10 July. As the solemn Session had been fixed for 15 July Morone was worried about possible last-minute hitches. He therefore suggested that the discussion of c. 1 should be remitted to a later date. He got the support of the Cardinal of Lorraine and the vast majority of the bishops.

On 15 July Session XXIII took place in an atmosphere of calm. The decrees put to the Assembly were approved without serious opposition. The text relating to episcopal residence took the place of what was before canon 1, the discussion of which had been postponed to a later date.

The debate on the appointment of bishops, which was the whole point of canon 1 of the new reform decree, was resumed on 11 September. The Cardinal of Lorraine and the Bishop of Verdun pleaded for a return to the election of bishops by the clergy, but did not turn down the project as a whole. Most of the French bishops took the same line.

After this first debate a commission was set up to revise the project. Of the 18 members of this commission 10 were Italian but only 2 French.

The second debate took place on 2 November. The Bishop of Segovia severely criticised the new text for its tendency in favour of the position taken by the curia. In their *votum* the Cardinal of Lorraine and the Archbishop of Braga praised the pope and in front of all stated that the pope wanted to bring about the reform. In spite of this the Cardinal of Lorraine remained a supporter of the freedom claimed by the Gallicans. It was in these circumstances that c. 1 of the reform decree was approved in the XXIVth Session of the Council of Trent.

And so the Tridentine texts on episcopal appointments came to be approved by vote. They are part of a concept of the priesthood defined exclusively by its sacramental function seen as the power to consecrate the Eucharist and to absolve sins.

No doubt c. 4 of the reform decree stresses the preaching of the Word of God as the main function of the bishop. The fact remains that the constant wavering of the Council between papalism and Gallicanism, presbyterialism and episcopalism, has led to an excessively 'priestly' interpretation of the ministry.

At Trent the conciliar Fathers were quite well aware of what a narrow view they had taken of the whole business. The result, however, of this game has been that post-Tridentine theology has been ingrained for several centuries with this lopsided sacralising view of the ministry, and that there was no protest by any Catholic theologians.

It is obvious that with a ministry interpreted in this way the laity have only an extremely limited role to play in the choice of their own bishops. The Church's ministers, indeed, are not seen rising from the grassroots community but rather as descending to the community from on high.

At the time of the Council of Trent there was hardly another way in which the Church could meet the challenge thrown down by the Calvinists and the Lutherans. At that moment in time it seemed imperative that the Church's ministers once again should constitute an *acies ordinata*. Nevertheless, it all shows why there has been no genuine theological dialogue between Catholicism and Lutheranism until Vatican II.

*Translated by T. L. Westow*

Notes

1. For this historical development, see V. Martin 'Le Choix des évêques dans l'Eglise latine' *Rev. Sc. Rel.* 4 (1924) 221-264; J. Gaudemet *Les Élections dans l'Eglise Latine* (Paris 1979).

2. Can. 329, 2 and 3.

3. The old elections were very different from what they have become in modern times. See J. Gaudemet, the article cited in note 1, 8-9.

4. Cf. Hefele-Leclercq *Histoire des conciles* 10, I p. 493 and pp. 565-567.

5. *Concilium Tridentinum. Diariorum, actorum, epistolarum, tractatuum nova collectio*, ed. by the Societas goerresiana (Frieburg i.B.) IX pp. 190lff; H. Jedin *Geschichte des Konzils von Trient* IV, pt. 2.

# PART II

*Theology*

Patrick Granfield

# The *Sensus Fidelium* in Episcopal Selection

'LAYPERSONS have always been enemies of the clergy.' With these words, Boniface VIII, in his characteristic bluntness, began the bull *Clericos Laicos*.[1] Nearly seven hundred years later, Vatican II, in a vastly different spirit, called the lay apostolate 'a participation in the saving mission of the Church itself' (*Lumen Gentium,* § 33). The Council stressed the right and responsibility of all the faithful to participate as fully as possible in the life of the Church. Certainly one of the most important events in the life of the local church is the selection of its chief pastor, teacher, liturgist, and administrator—the bishop. The process of selection is a serious one that demands great care and concern.

Today many Catholics feel that they do not have a sufficient voice in choosing their leaders. The current law of the Church dealing with norms for the selection of candidates for the episcopacy was issued in 1972 with the approval of Pope Paul VI. It allowed for a limited consultation process but, in the view of many canonists, it 'was still too restrictive, and did not seem to reflect the awakening consciousness of the responsible People of God in the Church'.[2]

The purpose of this article is to show that the active participation of the faithful (both the ordained and the non-ordained) in the selection of bishops is theologically sound. Our focal point is the *sensus fidelium* in its sacramental and pneumatic dimensions. We shall not discuss the possible practical models for episcopal selection but, rather, attempt to formulate a coherent theological rationale for vigorous lay and clerical involvement in the decisional process.

## 1. THE MEANING OF THE *SENSUS FIDELIUM*

The term *sensus fidelium* has a venerable tradition in Christian theology. From the patristic era up to the present, it appears in several different forms: *sensus* or *consensus fidelium, sensus fidei, sensus catholicus,* and *sensus Ecclesiae*. In general, it refers to the presence of a graced sensitivity in the faithful to the reality of sacred tradition. More precisely, Yves Congar describes it as 'the grace of faith in the *fidelis*, or religious subject, the quasi-instinctive ability that faith has to see and adhere to its object'.[3] John Henry Newman referred to it as 'a sort of instinct, or *phronema* deep in the bosom of the mystical body of Christ'.[4] The idea in both of these authors is that the *sensus fidelium* is present corporately within the community of believers as an intuition or understanding of the faith. It enables members of the Church to perceive God's revelation and the Church's teaching as consonant with divine truth. This ability or charism of discernment is given to the whole Church by the Holy Sprit and is one way, among many others, by which the faithful witness to the faith and discover the tradition of the Church.

Theologians, for the most part, discuss the *sensus fidelium* when they deal with infallibility or the prophetic ministry of Christians.[5] They point out that this instinct for authentic teaching should be seen as a spiritual deepening of the faith and not as an act which legally ratifies the teaching of the *magisterium*. Thus, Vatican II stated that the whole People of God cannot err in matters of faith: 'Thanks to a supernatural sense of faith (*sensus fidei*) which characterises the people as a whole, it manifests this unerring quality when "from the bishops down to the last member of the laity", it shows universal agreement in matters of faith and morals' (*Lumen Gentium* § 12).

It seems legitimate, however, also to use *sensus fidelium* to refer to a consultation with the faithful in other matters that affect the life of the community. There is ample historical and theological justification for this usage. Cyprian (d. 258), for example, insisted on receiving the advice and consent of the clergy and people before reaching a decision, since 'it behooves a bishop not only to teach but to learn'.[6] Paulinus of Nola (d. 431) said: 'Let us hang on the lips of all the faithful, because the Spirit of God breathes in every believer.'[7] Likewise, Newman's 'cooperation of the bishops and the faithful' (*pastorum et fidelium conspiratio*) envisioned a broad spectrum of interaction between the clergy and the laity.[8] Finally, the *sensus fidelium* was acknowledged in a practical manner in the centuries-long custom of the popular election of bishops. The procedure, which included the *testimonium, suffragium,* and *iudicium* of the entire community, recognised the right and value of the People of God to participate in episcopal elections.[9]

The *sensus fidelium* is above all a spiritual quality; it is not merely a counting of heads. Care should be taken that any use of it in episcopal selection should not be excessively juridical to the neglect of other prophetic manifestations in the Christian assembly. We should neither overestimate the judgment and holiness of the laity, many of whom in fact are only marginally related to the Church, nor should be underestimate the genuine presence of the Holy Spirit within the laity. Newman gives us the ideal: 'I want a laity not arrogant, not rash in speech, not disputatious, but men who know their religion, who enter into it, who know just where they stand, who know what they hold, and what they do not, who know their creed so well, that they can give an account of it, who know so much of history that they can defend it.'[10]

## 2. THE SACRAMENTAL BASIS

Essential to a full understanding of the *sensus fidelium* is its sacramental basis. Vatican II develops the teaching of St Thomas that 'the Church of Christ is constituted and built through faith and the sacraments of faith'.[11] The Council, relying heavily on sacred scripture, describes the Church as the 'new People of God', a 'messianic people', and a 'fellowship of life, charity, and truth' in which baptism is a constitutive element. *Lumen Gentium*, especially in Chapters 1, 2 and 4, presents the Church as community of laity, clergy, and religious, who are united in faith and the sacraments and have a common task of acting as the sign and instrument of Christ in the world.

The laity, then, 'share a common dignity from their rebirth in Christ' and 'share a true equality with regard to the dignity and to the activity of all the faithful for the building up of the Body of Christ' (*Lumen Gentium* § 32). It is through baptism and confirmation that the laity participate in the priestly, prophetic, and kingly functions of Christ.

Co-responsibility, as is evident from the above, was a predominant theme at Vatican II. In stressing the basic sacramental equality and dignity of the entire worshipping community, it laid the foundation for ecclesial democratisation and made lay participation in the election of bishops a natural consequence. Of special importance is the insistence of the Council on the 'true equality' of the laity, the *'plebs sancta'*. The Church is that community of believers called by God and not one formed on the basis of prior merit or holiness. The Church is a *communio* of love in which all share the following elements: one Lord, one Spirit, one faith, one baptism, one Word, one call to holiness, one heritage, and one common mission and ministry. The emphasis, clearly, is on the essential equality of the People of God; elitism and separatism are rejected.

If all the baptised are in the People of God and if there exists a fundamental equality among all—granting, of course, unique competencies—is there any reason why mature and responsible members of the Church should not participate in the selection of bishops? Pragmatic difficulties aside, there seems to be no overriding ecclesiological or sacramental argument that would militate against this. More positively, the voice of the laity, the *sensus fidelium*, should have a significant role in the decisional process that leads to the selection of the chief shepherd of the local Eucharistic assembly.

### 3. THE CHARISMATIC ASPECT

The charismatic or pneumatic dimension of the *sensus fidelium* also deserves our attention, because the intuitive or connatural response of believers to the faith is ultimately rooted in the activity of the Holy Spirit. The Church is, in the words of Cyprian, that 'people made one with the unity of the Father, the Son, and the Holy Spirit'.[12] The Spirit dwells in the hearts of the faithful, makes the Church his creation, and guides it in the unity of fellowship. The Spirit, moreover, 'distributes special graces among the faithful of every rank' (*Lumen Gentium* § 12). These gifts or *charismata* enable the recipient to perform a unique ministry within the Church. St Paul writes: 'In each of us the Sprit is manifested in one particular way, for some useful purpose' (I Cor. 12:7). The charisms are functional graces primarily directed to the upbuilding of the Church. As such, they are not meant to be possessed but to be used. The Christian has a duty and a responsibility to exercise his charisms and by so doing becomes 'a witness and a living instrument of the mission of the Church itself' (*Lumen Gentium* § 33).

Charisms can be considered as concrete expression of the *sensus fidelium*—gifts that manifest the presence of the Sprit and contribute to the growth and sanctification of the Body of Christ which is the Church. If properly understood and exercised, charisms strengthen the unity of the Church. Since both the hierarchy and the laity are given unique gifts, their ordering and mutual recognition is essential. 'There is,' as St Paul reminds us, 'a variety of gifts, but always the same Spirit' (I Cor. 12:4). The charisms of the laity are not derived from the hierarchy but exist in their own right. Shared responsibility and collegial interaction are marks of the charismatic community. The observation of Jürgen Moltmann is well taken: 'It [the Church] must stop being a Church of ministers functioning on behalf of laymen, and become a charismatic fellowship in which everyone recognises his ministry and lays hold of his charism.'[13]

The selection of bishops is linked to the exercise of charisms. The Church is composed of many persons who share a plurality of gifts or ministries. No single group, however, can claim to have a monopoly on the gifts of the Spirit. Because of the presence of charisms, all levels of Church membership—laity, clergy, and religious—should be allowed to participate in the choosing of bishops in the local church. The local church is, after all, the Church—the place where the Church is made present and becomes event. The competence of the local church should not be ignored. The members of the local church best know their own needs; can contribute their particular charisms and insights; and can act responsibly in choosing someone as their leader. The selection of a bishop is à delicate and critical act of discernment—which is itself a charism; the entire community should take part in it. 'One cannot speak of the co-responsibility of the laity, if participation in decision-making is excluded.'[14]

## 4. SOME CLARIFICATIONS

Lay participation in the life of the Church has increased dramatically since Vatican II. There is undoubtedly a heightened consciousness in the body of the faithful regarding their proper role in the ecclesial community. The laity, more and more, have become influential agents of change within the Church and have perceived with remarkable clarity their unique responsibility. Three general areas of involvement may be mentioned. First, the liturgical reform mandated by the Council encouraged greater lay participation. The use of the vernacular, the renewed rites and modern translations of the texts, and a broad catechetical effort have produced significant results. Second, the laity have also been active in many Church-related activities: the charismatic movement; diocesan offices; extra-canonical communities, especially the *communidades de base*; mission work; pastoral and team ministries; theological teaching; and social justice organisations. Third, certain non-hierarchical decision-making bodies have appeared: priests' and sisters' senates; parish and diocesan councils; and, in some countries, national pastoral synods. There is developing, in effect, a kind of ecclesiology 'from below' and it is not being accomplished without trial and error, painful tensions, and considerable anguish.

The primary intent of this article has been to suggest a greater role for the People of God in the selection of bishops. For some, such a prospect is a sign of hope; for others, it is the source of concern, at times bordering on alarm. In order to minimise the latter reaction and to balance our ealier arguments, three clarifications seem appropriate.

First, to suggest that the entire community elect its bishop is not a blind return to the past. Nostalgia or Utopianism are not adequate reasons for the present re-introduction of such a practice. This would be archaism which idealises the past—if it is old, it is good—it fails to take into account the great differences that exist between the early and modern Church. One cannot equate the third-century diocese of Carthage with the twentieth-century diocese of Paris. It is unreasonable to imitate uncritically all the customs of an earlier era.

A more fruitful approach to the past is one which attempts to discover the richness in the tradition and to discern the decisive and abiding truth that lies behind certain patterns and practices. By using our historical consciousness and by critically analysing tradition, it is possible to identify some convincing reasons for the popular election of bishops. Thus, we find the recognition of the Church as a *communio*, a fellowship of believers; the insistence on the sacramental equality and dignity of all Christians; the idea of a universal priesthood and the presence of *charismata*; the freedom of the children of God; and the acceptance of the collegial ideal. These and similar reasons attest to a vital *sensus fidelium* and they are still valid today. Furthermore, history also reveals that the changes in the electoral practices were due not to theological reasons but to cultural ones: the decline of an educated laity; abuses in the form of intrigue, bribery, and violence; and interference of secular rulers in Church affairs.

The task of the present Church is to reflect on the lessons of history and to develop new patterns for the selection of bishops which would incorporate the insights of the past and would be properly accommodated to the needs of the modern Christian. The result would not be a carbon copy of the past but one that would provide a genuine role for the voice of the clergy and laity. A general plebescite would obviously be unfeasible. The proposal, however, of the Canon Law Society of America which suggests that bishops be selected by a representative diocesan committee has considerable merit.[15]

Second, there is no absolute guarantee that a more democratic election procedure will always produce the most qualified candidate. The same caveat, however, could also be said of the present system. It is a truism that there exists no perfect system of ecclesial election; every system has its advantages and disadvantages. The aphorism of Kierkegaard, 'The majority is always wrong,' must be weighed against the observation of Pope Leo I: 'He who is in charge of all, should be chosen by all.'

The success of any electoral system in the Church that involves a broadly based representative body depends ultimately, of course, on the promised assistance of the Spirit but proximately, on the sincerity, Christian maturity, and commitment of the electors. Practical but vexing questions include: Who should have voting rights? How should the system be structured? What canonical force should be given to such elections? And what are the respective competencies in the process of the laity, clergy, religious, provincial bishops, and pope? All these matters deserve serious attention. Granting the possibility of collective errors in such a system, nevertheless, it seems that an efficient, democratic voting procedure has much to recommend it. It would foster the responsibility of the laity, increase credibility and ecclesial identity, express and strengthen the sense of *communio*, introduce a much needed element of accountability, and relate the bishop more closely with his people.

Third, it does not follow that to suggest the popular election of bishops is to view the Church as a democracy, either direct or indirect (representative). The Church is not, nor should it be, a democracy; the overwhelming testimony of sacred scripture and tradition in no way suggests that the people possess the power and transmit it to their representatives.[16] Church government is unique. Although it is true, as Robert Bellarmine pointed out in *De controversiis*, that there are monarchic, aristrocratic, and democratic elements in the Church, we cannot adequately describe the Church by models taken from political theory. Nevertheless, it is possible to encourage democratic forms within Church structure and to speak of ecclesial democratisation. If a bishop were elected by the people, he would not be simply their spokesman or representative in a legal sense. Bishops are not called 'vicars of the Roman Pontiff', but shepherds 'who exercise an authority which is proper to them' (*Lumen Gentium* § 27). So too, if elected by the community, bishops would not be vicars of the people but rather would govern the Church in the name of Christ.

In conclusion, the selection of bishops by members of the local ecclesial community is a most important aspect of contemporary Church reform—an honest attempt to allow mature men and women of the People of God to share more intimately in the mission of the Church. In presenting the theological reasons for such collegial activity, we have used the concept of the *sensus fidelium*. This ancient idea, although usually doctrinally focused, can, we suggest, also be properly applied to the more practical matter of the choosing of Church leaders. It is, above all, a charismatic gift, rooted in faith and the sacraments; it assists the faithful in discerning the presence of the Spirit and in responding to his guidance. Active participation of the faithful in episcopal selection would be a significant and desirable manifestation of the Spirit who 'guides the Church into the fullness of truth and gives her a unity of fellowship and service' (*Lumen Gentium* § 4).

*Notes*

1. 25 February 1296 (*Magnum Bullarium Romanum* [1741], IX, 110).
2. D. E. Heintschel in Foreword to *Procedure for the Selection of Bishops in the United States. A Suggested Implementation of Present Papal Norms* (Document from the Canon Law Society of America, 1973), p. ii.
3. *Lay People in the Church* (Westminster Md. 1957) p. 275 (*Jalons pour une théologie du laicat*, 2nd ed. [Paris 1954] p. 398). This book is still the most thorough and perceptive study we have on the theology of the laity. Congar also discusses the *sensus fidelium* in *Tradition and Traditions* (New York 1967). (*La tradition et les traditions* [Paris 1960]).
4. *On Consulting the Faithful in Matters of Doctrine*, ed. J. Coulson (New York 1961) p. 73.
5. See S. Femiano *Infallibility of the Laity* (New York 1967); W. M. Thompson '*Sensus Fidelium* and Infallibility' *American Ecclesiastical Review* 167 (1973) 450-486; and J. T. Ford 'Newman on "*Sensu Fidelium*" and Mariology' *Marian Studies* 28 (1977) 120-145.
6. *Ep.* 74, 10 (*Corpus scriptorum ecclesiasticorum latinorum* [1871] 2, 807). Hereafter cited as *CSEL*. See P. Granfield, 'Consilium and Consensus: Decision-Making in Cyprian' *The Jurist* 35 (1975) 397-408.
7. *Ep.* 23, 36 (*CSEL* Hartel [1894] 29, 193).
8. In the work cited in note 4, p. 104.
9. See R. Eno 'Shared Responsibility in the Early Church' *Chicago Studies* 9 (1970) 129-141; W. Bassett ed. *The Choosing of Bishops* (Hartford 1971), especially articles by R. P. McBrien 'A Preliminary Ecclesiological Statement' pp. 11-20, and T. F. O'Meara 'Emergence and Decline of Popular Voice in the Selection of Bishops' pp. 21-32; J. E. Lynch 'Co-responsibility in the first Five Centuries: Presbyterial Colleges and the Election of Bishops' *The Jurist* 31 (1971) 14-53; J. M. Torrents *Las elecciones episcopales en la historia de la iglesia* (Barcelona 1972); G. Alberigo and A. Weiler, eds. *Elections and Consensus in the Church, Concilium* 77 (American edition) (New York 1971); P. Granfield 'Episcopal Elections in Cyprian: Clerical and Lay Participation' *Theological Studies* 37 (1976) 41-52; and J. Gaudemet et al. *Les Élections dans l'Eglise latine des origines au XVIe siècle* (Paris 1979).
10. *Lectures on the Present Position of Catholics in England* (London n.d.), Lecture 9, 4, p. 390.
11. *Summa theologiae* 3a Q.64, art. 2 ad 3. F. Klosterman gives an excellent commentary on Ch. 4 of *Lumen Gentium* and *Apostolicam Actuositatem* (Decree on the Laity) in *Commentary on the Documents of Vatican II* (New York 1967/69) I pp. 231-252 and III pp. 273-404. (*Das Zweite Vatikanische Konzil. Konstitutionen, Dekrete, und Erklärungen* [Freiburg 1966/67] I pp. 260-283 and II pp. 585-701.
12. *De Oratione Dominica* 23 (*CSEL* Hartel [1868] 1 p. 285).
13. *The Church in the Power of the Spirit* (New York 1975) p. 242. (*Kirche in der Kraft des Geistes* [München 1975] p. 268).
14. N. Greinacher 'Das Vollzug der Kirche im Bistum' in *Handbuch der Pastoraltheologie* (Freiburg 1968) III 106. Also H. Küng 'Participation of the Laity in Church Leadership and in Church Elections' *Journal of Ecumenical Studies* 6 (1969) 511-533.
15. See the document cited in note 2. Cf. J.-L. Harouel *Les désignations épiscopales dans le droit contemporain* (Paris 1977).
16. See P. Granfield *Ecclesial Cybernetics: A Study of Democracy in the Church* (New York 1973) and A. Müller, ed. *Democratization in the Church, Concilium* 63 (American edition) (New York 1971).

# Edward Kilmartin

# Episcopal Election:
# The Right of the Laity

TWENTIETH-CENTURY Roman Catholic ecclesiologists are said to have redis-
covered that the particular episcopal church is truly Church and not a part of Church.
Perhaps it is closer to the truth to speak of the recovery of an important consequence of
the ecclesial nature of the particular church, namely, that it is subject of rights. The
Second Vatican Council received this teaching and so provided support for those
engaged in rethinking the role of the Bishop or Rome in the communion of churches. In
this connection, the style of exercise of papal authority in the matter of nomination of
bishops within the Latin Church is being called into question. It has a legal basis (CIC,
cn. 329, 2) grounded on the solemn declaration of First Vatican Council's *Pastor
Aeternus* which affirms the immediate jurisdiction of the pope over individual churches
(*singulas ecclesias*).[1] But it is more consistent with a universalist ecclesiology than with a
communion ecclesiology.

The Second Vatican Council also received Roman Catholic theology's rediscovery
of the theology of co-responsibility of the laity for the mission of the Church. This
initiated a discussion in the Council itself about the possible inclusion of laity in the
episcopal election process.[2] After the Council this topic has received some attention.[3]
There is a seemingly widespread agreement among scholars that laity should have an
advisory role in this matter. But are they capable of right of election along with clergy?
The history of episcopal elections of the churches of East and West shows that laity were
involved in a variety of ways and that the inclusion or exclusion of lay election right was
based on shifting theological grounds.

## 1. HISTORY OF THE THEOLOGY OF LAY RIGHT OF ELECTION

In the undivided Church of the first four centuries the participation of the laity,
where it occurred, was considered an integral part of the spiritual event which included
election, ordination and reception of the newly ordained bishop.[4] The subsequent
restriction of election right, in the East to bishops[5] and in the West to a wider circle of
clergy,[6] was designed to curb the unspiritual interference of lay powers in canonical
elections. The theological justification for this was generally sought in the authority of
tradition. The Second Council of Nicaea appealed, however incorrectly, to cn. 4 of the

39

First Council of Nicaea (325). In the West when the role of laity in elections was being played down, Gratian, the father of modern canon law, favoured the principle that elections belong to the clergy and consent to the laity in his *Decretum* (ca. 1140).[7] This was based on his reading of the history of election practice. However, the twelfth-century decretists allowed exceptions to this principle; some even thought that clergy could award election right to laity. They assume that election right is not anchored in ordination to the clerical state.[8]

## 2. JURISDICTIONAL AUTHORITY OF LAITY

The theological grounds for the decretists' position is not available to twentieth-century Roman Catholic theologians. Developments in the theology of ordained ministry have led to the consensus that presbyterial and episcopal ordination involves the bestowal of both power of order (to celebrate sacraments) and pastoral power (to teach and govern) as complementary aspects of office. The Second Vatican Council received this teaching and so speaks in several places of the 'holy power' which qualifies the 'ministerial priesthood' in the spheres of worship, teaching and government.[9] If pastoral office is communicated through ordination does it follow that laity are incapable of a limited share in pastoral authority, including episcopal election right?

In the post-conciliar period Klaus Mörsdorf, the influential German canon lawyer, and others, have developed a theological argument which excludes the laity from any exercise of pastoral authority.[10] Here the Church is conceived as universal sacrament of salvation, hierarchically structured to reveal its mystery. Christ the invisible head of the body is symbolically rendered visible through the heads of the Church who are given a share in the leadership service by ordination and so enabled to act in his name and power. Because the spiritual and juridical Church are so interlocked, leadership in the Church includes powers over worship, teaching and government. These powers are not separable for they are only aspects of the one only power through the exercise of which Christ the head is symbolically present and active as the principal agent.

Laity, who have not received the consecration to represent Christ the head, are incapable of acting in his name and power in a leadership capacity. The attempt to attribute to them a limited share in pastoral authority militates against the Catholic concept of hierarchical authority by removing its sacramental basis.

There is another way of looking at the question of the laity's capacity for pastoral authority. It begins with the understanding of the Church as a communion of those who live in Christ through the Spirit and in which each one has a measure of gifts to share with the others. Thus Ulrich Mosiek, another German canon lawyer, speaks of a more comprehensive pastoral authority derived from ordination. It includes certain activities which in the practice of the Church have always been reserved to the ordained. But there are areas of Church life in which the baptised have been commissioned to exercise limited pastoral authority. Musiek points out that through the rite of initiation believers are incorporated into the Church and so assume responsibility for the apostolate both within and outside of the community of believers. While their mission is more normally carried on through the witness of a good life, they can be drawn into the hierarchical apostolate in accord with the needs of the Church and their particular qualifications.[11]

## 3. RELATION OF LAITY TO HIERARCHY IN THE SECOND VATICAN COUNCIL

The Second Vatican Council provides two lines of thought to which the advocates of the preceding positions can appeal. In a series of statements, untempered by

pneumato-ecclesiological considerations, bishops and priests are described as par-
ticipants in the priesthood of Christ, or recipients of a holy power which enables them to
act in the person of Christ. Thus, for example, priests are said 'to share in the hierarchical priesthood of Christ',[12] rather than in the hierarchical ministry established by
Christ through the personal mission of the Holy Spirit to the Church. In these instances
the hierarchical minister appears to be a sacred representative of Christ set apart from
the people and definable almost exclusively in relation to Christ the head.

On the other hand, the ordained minister is also described as one who is installed in
an office of the Church and who receives the gift of the Holy Spirit to fulfil this
function.[13] In this case the ordained is understood to participate in the Holy Spirit whom
Christ sent to the whole Church. His ministry is a 'ministry of the Church itself'.[14] It does
not absorb all ministries. On the contrary, while he can be called pastor or father, he
must also be considered servant and steward who facilitates the ministries of all. This
perspective indicates that a very close relationship exists between the ministries of laity
and hierarchy.

The Second Vatican Council does attempt to establish the connection between the
ministries of laity and hierarchy. But the christocentric understanding of ordained
ministry prevails. While the laity are awarded an advisory role in matters effecting
Church life, stress is placed on the reverent attitude they should show for those who
'represent the person of Christ' and obedience to 'the pastors who . . . represent Christ'.
The analogy is even introduced between Christ's obedience to the Father and that of the
laity to the hierarchy.[15] The overall description of the inner-church ministry takes the
form of an *Ein-Mann-System* with the laity being directed to a ministry 'before the
world'.[16]

#### 4. BEYOND THE SECOND VATICAN COUNCIL: A TRINITARIAN VIEW OF CHRISTIAN MINISTRY

Because of its Christocentric orientation the Second Vatican Council was unable to
show how the ministries of laity and ordained grow out of the mystery of the priestly
People of God without the one being simply under the control of the other. The ordering
of these ministries to one another can best be shown from a systematic presentation
which begins with a consideration of the Holy Trinity in the economy of salvation.

The Father, who sent the Son, also sends the Holy Spirit through the Risen Lord.
Personally co-missioned with the Church to carry on the mission which Jesus began
during his earthly life, the Holy Spirit inspires believers to engage in the work of the
gospel and instils that life of faith in others whereby they respond to the preaching of the
Good News.

By virtue of the Spirit's personal mission the Church is fully constituted as sacrament
of salvation, as II Vatican Council states.[17] Thus as 'sign and instrument of intimate
union with God and of the unity of the whole human race'[18] in the power of the Spirit,
the Church can be described as sacrament of the Spirit. Still because the Spirit's mission
derives from Christ and has a completely Christ-ward reference, it can also be named 'a
kind of sacrament in Christ'[19] or sacrament of Christ in the Spirit.

Within the Spirit-filled Church authorisation for a leadership function takes place
through a spiritual event which includes election, ordination and reception of the newly
ordained. The whole process denotes incorporation into a ministry of the Church,
something that can be lived. The human and social meaning connotes, in turn, for the
eyes of faith the reception of the abiding support of the Spirit. This is expressed in the
central prayer of the rite of ordination which in all liturgies refers to the gift of the Spirit.

The authorisation for public ministry in the Church, therefore, takes place through
the Church and the Holy Spirit. But these sources of authority should not be viewed as

D

operating independently of one another. The Church authorises the candidate in the power of the Spirit who works through the Church.

The same structure is present in the activity of the ordained. As member of the Church the ordained minister can only directly represent the Church. The exercise of jurisdictional power by the official representatives of the juridical Church connotes for those who live in the Spirit the activity of the Holy Spirit. By way of a kind of 'appropriation' this activity of the Holy Spirit is typically referred to Christ the head of the Church in a Latin christomonistic frame of reference. Still the activity of the hierarchy is more correctly seen as a manifestation of the action of the Spirit, since he is source of all spiritual authority in the Church.

Since the spiritual authority of the laity derives from fidelity to the inspirations of the same Spirit, it does not seem necessary to confine every jurisdictional-ecclesiastical representation of the Church to the ordained.

The baptised are incapable of assuming pastoral authority which embraces the full scope of permanent ministry of leadership. A commissioning of this sort would imply that ordination is dispensable: a purely ceremonial rite. There are also certain activities which, by their nature, require ordained ministry lest the hierarchical structure of the Church be obscured. Among these are many of those concentrated expressions of the mystery of the Church and its stable juridical structures known as sacraments. Thus laity cannot lead the celebration of the Lord's Supper, the most profound manifestation and realisation of Church.[20] Otherwise a limited share of the laity in pastoral authority which takes place in communion with the hierarchy is excluded if it can be shown to be contrary to the will of Christ the head.

To establish this thesis a Christocentric view of the ordained ministry is often introduced. It appears to be modelled on a platonic or neo-platonic concept of symbol wherein the historical appearance, detached from a communitarian relation, serves as transparency for supra-mundane realities. This is linked to biblical sayings about Christ's promise to be with his apostles in their ministry and to the image of the Church as a body of which Christ is head. Through this Christological short-circuit the ordained are depicted as sharing in 'Christ's Spirit', i.e., in the Spirit of the Risen Lord as distinguished from the Holy Spirit. They are thus placed over against the Church rather than with the Church over against the world, i.e., humankind in need of the gospel.

This presentation is unsatisfactory within a Trinitarian perspective which situates the Holy Spirit between Christ the head and the Church as principle of union and source of the Church's spiritual authority. From this standpoint it does not seem to be theologically incorrect to entertain the thought that laity can be introduced into the decision-making process in the Church in instances such as the election of bishops which, by their very nature, are not calculated to undermine the essential hierarchical structure of the Church. It goes without saying that clergy should be included in the electoral body since they constitute an essential aspect of the operational structures of the Church. But norms which a priori exclude laity seem hardly defensible, at least in so far as based on a preference for a Christocentric rather than Trinitarian concept of Church and ministry.

*Notes*

1. D.S. 3064.
2. In the final formulation of *Christus Dominus* 20, which deals with episcopal elections, the wish is expressed that various forms of participation by civil authorities be terminated. However, as the history of this passage shows, other forms of lay participation were deliberately not excluded (see H. Müller 'Der Anteil der Laien an der Bischofswahl: Ein Beitrag zur Geschichte der Kanonistik von Gratian bis Gregor IX' *Kanonistische Studien und Texte 29* B. R. Grüner (Amsterdam 1977) 228-232.
3. See L. and A. Swidler, eds. *Bishops and People* (Philadelphia, Westminster 1970) (Translation of *Theologische Quartalschrift* 149 [2, 1969]); W. W. Bassett, ed. *The Choosing of Bishops* (Canon Law Society of America Historical and Theological Studies) (Hartford, Conn. 1971); G. Alberigo and A. Weiler, eds. *Election and Consent in the Church* (*Concilium* 77) (New York 1972); H. Müller, the article cited in the preceding note 235-250.
4. For a summary of the early history of lay involvement in episcopal elections, see H. Müller, the article cited in note 2, 9-22.
5. II Council of Nicaea (787), cn. 3, restricts election to bishops.
6. The movement to exclude laity from episcopal election reached a climax when Gregory IX (1227-1241) declared invalid elections involving laity.
7. *Decretum Gratiani* D.62 pr.
8. H. Müller, the article cited in note 2, 209-210.
9. E.g., *Lumen Gentium* § 10.
10. K. Mörsdorf 'Das Weihesakrament in seiner Tragweite für den verfassungsrechtlichen Aufbau der Kirche' *Ephemerides theologicae Lovanienses* 52 (1976) 193-204; K. Peters 'Die doppelte Repräsentation als verfassungsrechtliches Structurelement der Kirche' *Trierer Theologische Zeitschrift* 86 (1977) 228-234.
11. U. Musiek 'Der Laien als Jurisdiktionsträger?' *Österreichisches Archiv für Kirchenrecht* 25 (1974) 3-15.
12. *Optatam totius* § 2.
13. *Lumen Gentium* § 20-21.
14. *Presbyterorum ordinis* § 15.
15. *Lumen Gentium* § 37.
16. *Lumen Gentium* § 38.
17. *Lumen Gentium* § 48.
18. *Lumen Gentium* § 1.
19. *Lumen Gentium* § 1.
20. *Lumen Gentium* § 11.

Joseph Lécuyer

# The Bishop and the People in the Rite of Episcopal Consecration

THE RITE of episcopal consecration was instituted by the Apostolic Constitution *Pontificalis Romani* on 18 June 1968. It departs in many respects from the previous Roman Pontifical, but it still contains elements that go back to a very early date, in particular those concerned with the part played by the people in the election and consecration. It is these elements that we shall attempt to evaluate here.

### 1. THE PARTICIPATION OF THE PEOPLE IN THE CONSECRATION

The general principle is stated at the beginning of the document: 'The episcopal consecration will take place with the participation of the believing people' (*Pontificalis Romani* 1). Elsewhere, the document states that attempts must be made to ensure 'better participation on the part of the faithful' and to set out the seats 'so that the faithful can be properly associated with the whole liturgical action' (*PR* 9). This is certainly in accordance with the earliest tradition of the Church—according to the ritual of Hippolytus of Rome, 'the people will gather together with the presbyterium and the bishops who are present', a requirement that is taken up again by Book VIII (4, 3) of the Apostolic Constitutions. Origen also insisted on the presence of the people at the consecration of a bishop.[1] There are many references, in the early liturgical books, to the prayer of the whole people. One in particular, from the *Missale Francorum*, is worth mentioning here: 'May we receive the unanimous help of the prayer of all; may the prayer of all be directed towards the one who receives the heavy burden to pray for all'.[2] The consecration of a bishop, then, is clearly the concern of the whole Christian community.

### 2. THE PRESENTATION OF THE NEWLY ELECTED BISHOP

The entrance procession is followed in the Pontifical by a short dialogue. One of the priests present turns to the principal consecrating bishop and says to him: 'Father, the Church of N. asks you to consecrate the priest here present for the responsibility of the episcopate' (*PR* 16). Several representatives of the church concerned may then express the expectations of the diocese or present the candidate who has already been named to members of his future diocese.

The principal consecrator's reply is very illuminating: 'You must have received from the pope the letter naming him for this task. Let it be read aloud.' After it has been read, all that those present have to do is to give their assent—they all say: *'Deo gratias' (PR* 17). The people, then, only have to consent to a nomination or an election that has already been made by the pope. That is the situation at present in the West.

It has, however, not always been like this. A perusal of the early liturgies of the Church reveals that, in accordance with changing circumstances, the choice of a new bishop was for a very long time entrusted to the whole of the Christian community, the clergy or the bishops of the province. In the *Apostolic Tradition* of Hippolytus, for example, the newly elected bishop had to be chosen and accepted by all the people.[3] According to the *Statuta Ecclesiae Antiqua*, compiled at the end of the fifth century, the consent of the clergy and the laity was required.[4] Despite the obscurity of the text, the same can be said of the *Missale Francorum*. Between the eighth and the tenth centuries, the *Ordines Romani* continued to affirm that the whole Christian people had to take part in the election of the bishop and to present the candidate.[5] The principle of Celestine I was accepted as the norm: 'That no church should be given a bishop against its will; that enquiries may be made concerning the consent and the wish of the clergy, the people and the order (of bishops?)'.[6] This principle was quoted word for word in the tenth-century Romano-Germanic Pontifical[7].

In the East, at least according to the Apostolic Constitutions, the candidate was elected and presented by the presbyterium and the people.[8] Nonetheless, at the time when Origen was writing, some bishops named their successors. These were sometimes elected by neighbouring bishops. Sometimes the people were consulted, but very often 'he gives his favour under the influence of clamorous demands and even money'.[9] The first Council of Nicaea (325) decided (in canons 4 and 6) that only the provincial bishops could make the ultimate choice and that an election by the people would not be sufficient.[10] Certain Eastern rites have preserved a reference to the unanimous vote of the people[11], although the decisions made at the Councils of Antioch and Laodicea and confirmed by canon 22 of the Eighth Ecumenical Council [12] were accepted in practice. According to this canon, the choice was to be made by the synod of bishops, in order to avoid a possible intervention on the part of the secular authorities.

In the West, the clergy and the people continued in practice to elect their bishops for much longer. The dangers involved in this method were known, however, and in the seventh century the Pontifical of Besançon issued a warning against accepting certain persons and agains simony.[13] In the same way, the danger of promises made to electors was also denounced in the eighth-century *Ordo Romanus* 34.[14] Very gradually, the intervention of the secular powers came to play a more and more important part. According to the Magdalen College Pontifical of the twelfth century, for example, the election of the bishop was confined to the King of England 'with the consent of the clergy and the people'. This intervention of political power was to lead to those abuses of lay investiture that can be found in various forms in the Pontificals. Despite the Gregorian reform, confusion reigned until the Council of Trent.

### 3. THE EXAMINATION OF THE NEWLY ELECTED BISHOP

What may be called the 'examination' of the candidate takes place after the homily. This examination is introduced by the words: 'It is a very old rule of the Church that we should ask, *in the presence of the people*, the one who is going to become a bishop if he will commit himself to upholding the faith and to carrying out the duties of his task' (*PR*

19; the italics are mine). The whole community bears witness—this fact emerges quite clearly from the fifth-century *Statuta Ecclesiae Antiqua*[15] and the formula used in them was also employed in the Romano-Germanic Pontifical five hundred years later. This part played by the community was not, however, explicitly mentioned in the Roman Pontifical. The decision to draw attention to it once again was a happy one.

## 4. THE PRAYER OF CONSECRATION

The examination is followed by an invitation on the part of the consecrator to all the people to pray. After the litanies of the saints, everyone is united in the great prayer of consecration, which is derived from the very early text found in the *Apostolic Tradition* and preserved in several of the Eastern liturgies. I should like here to draw attention to these words: 'Father, *you who know the heart of man*, give to *the one whom you have chosen* . . .'.[16] I shall confine myself to two comments.

In the first place, whatever method is used to name the bishop in the human sense, he is clearly chosen by God. This divine choice goes beyond the interventions of the people, the clergy, the synod of bishops or the pope. The call to the episcopate and the grace and the powers of the bishop's ministry come from God.

Secondly, the words that I have emphasised (in italics) come from Acts 1:24. The election of Matthias would therefore seem to be taken as a point of reference for all later episcopal elections. In this context, it is worth noting that three interventions take place in the election of Matthias. Firstly, Peter speaks in the name of the Eleven and decides that Judas must be replaced. Secondly, the community presents two candidates. Thirdly, in response to everyone's prayer, God names the one chosen.

This model cannot be applied as it stands to the election of our bishops today, but the threefold structure can always be found in some form—the college of bishops intervenes decisively, the Christian community participates by presenting the candidates and uniting in prayer and finally a divine call is made manifest in the rite of consecration.

This final aspect is apparent in several formulae in the present liturgy. It is, for example, God who has joined the new bishop 'to Christ the sovereign priest' (*PR* 28). It is the Holy Spirit who has appointed him 'as a bishop to govern the Church of God' (*PR* 32; cf. Acts 20:28). Finally, it is the Lord who has appointed him as 'the shepherd of his people' (*PR* 39). In the East, there is an almost identical formula that occurs in all the rites and expresses this divine election: 'Divine grace . . . has chosen N. as bishop'.

## 5. SOME CONCLUSIONS

As Dom B. Botte wrote more than twenty years ago: 'Whatever means are used to name the person, it is divine grace that chooses him and this election is effective in the act of consecration and in the mediation of the members of the hierarchy'.[17] Nonetheless, God's choice can normally only be known 'in the signs by which the will of God is customarily made known to prudent Christians'.[18] Before consecrating, then, the bishops have to make this prudent discernment—the questions asked in the rite of consecration bear witness to this duty to find out about the abilities and the faith of the candidate. It may perhaps be said that these are purely ritual questions, but the fact remains that, if the candidate refuses to give a satisfactory reply, the consecrator has the right—and the duty—to interrupt the ceremony, even after the pope's letter has been read. It is clear from these facts, then, that the election of bishops still has an aspect of collegiality. At the same time, however, for reasons that cannot be discussed in this article, this aspect has become obscured, especially in the Western Church.

Similar comments can be made about the part played by the people in the choice of a new bishop. The Pontifical refers, for example, to the expectations of the people, their requests, the part that they play in the prayer, the examination and in the whole of the ceremony and so on. All this is meaningful only if the community has been consulted in some way and if the new bishop is not imposed on the community, in the words of Celestine I, 'against its will'.

How, then, should this consultation take place? Should the matter be put to the vote among the clergy, the leaders and the responsible members of the community? Who would have the courage to claim that any one method is necessarily the best? Surely no sociological analysis or legal arrangement is sufficient in any question where God's will has to be known!

Ambrose of Milan pointed out forcibly to the members of the church of Verceil that what they had to look for was God's choice, not the candidates' wishes or factions.[19] The texts of the Pontifical drew attention to the importance of prayer when God's will has to be known. According to Origen, 'whether it is the people, who often show their preference under the influence of propaganda (*clamoribus!*) or perhaps of money, or whether it is the bishops themselves, who will regard himself as able to make such a choice unless the Lord has revealed it to him in response to his prayer and his request?'[20] We may therefore conclude that it is to the Christian community praying around Peter and the Eleven that God, 'who knows the hearts of men', gives knowledge of 'the one whom he has chosen' so that the college of the apostles may be completed.[21]

*Translated by David Smith*

## Notes

1. Origen *In Leviticum Hom.* VI. 3 (ed. Baehrens I p. 363); see also *In Numeros Hom.* XXII. 4 (*id.* II, pp. 208-209).

2. See A. Santantoni *L'Ordinazione episcopale* (Rome 1976) p. 80.

3. *Traditio Apostolica* 2.

4. Ed. C. Munier (Paris 1960) p. 78.

5. *OR* 34, n. 14, 30, 38 (ed. Andrieu III p. 606 ff); *OR* 35 A. n. 6; *OR* 36, n. 35 (*id.*, IV, pp. 74 and 201).

6. Celestine I *Epist.* IV, c. 5 (*PL* 50. 434b). I have translated the word *ordo* here as 'order of bishops'. It is, however, possible that it may have been the *ordo* of the city magistrates.

7. Romano-Germanic Pontifical LXIII. 18 (eds. Vogel and Elze II p. 212).

8. Apostolic Constitutions VIII, 4, 2-3.

9. Origen *In Numeros Hom.* XXII. 4 (ed. Baehrens II p. 208 ff).

10. See the Council of Antioch (A.D. 341). canon 16; Council of Laodicea, canons 12-13, etc.

11. See H. Denzinger *Ritus Orientalium* II p. 18 etc.

12. Fourth Council of Constantinople (A.D. 869-870), canon 22.

13. Ed. Martène L. 1, c.8, a. 11, *ordo* 10 (II col. 154).

14. *OR* 34, n. 22 and 27.

15. Ed. Munier, p. 78, lin. 35-36.

16. These words are taken from Acts 1:24.

17. B. Botte *Etudes sur le Sacrement de l'Ordre, Lex Orandi* 22 (Paris 1957) p. 31.

18. Vatican II, Decree on the Ministry and Life of Priests *Presbyterorum ordinis* 11.

19. Ambrose *Epist.* 63. 48-49 (PL 16. 1253-1254).

20. Origen *In Numeros Hom.* XXII. 4 (ed. Baehrens II p. 208).

21. See Acts 1:24; these texts are included in the prayer of the consecration of a bishop.

Giovanni Cereti

# The Ecumenical Importance of the Laity's Collaboration in the Choice of Bishops

THE DOCUMENT on the 'ministry of vigilance and unity in the local Church' published in 1976 by the Dombes group begins by saying that the problem of the episcopate must not be approached only from the doctrinal angle, because the actual way in which it functions can be of decisive importance (no. 8). Among the proposals it then puts forward for the Catholic Church—for which it says a spirit of conversion is necessary (8 and 58)—is the suggestion that the whole people of God should be involved in the choice of bishops.

'The way in which bishops are chosen has changed a great deal in the history of the Catholic Church, and consequently the present practice of appointing them is neither unchangeable nor the only possible one. To show that episcopal authority is rooted in the communion of the Church, it is important that the appointment of a bishop should result from a living relationship between the Bishop of Rome, the neighbouring bishops, the priests of the diocese and all the Christian people concerned. We think it right that the whole people of God should be associated in the choice of its bishop.' (62)[1]

This text sums up well the reason why a greater involvement of the whole people of God is important from an ecumenical point of view. It is not only a question of returning to a practice which was common in the Church at the time when the present divisions had not yet arisen, or of coming closer to other Christian Churches who have kept the episcopate too. More importantly, it is an attempt to translate into facts an ecclesiology of communion, so that the reform of the Catholic Church demanded by Vatican II (UR 6) should be put into operation in this area. This reform was seen by the Council as an indispensable pre-condition for any action towards the re-establishment of full communion between all Christians.[2]

In this article we shall first examine the current practice in various Christian Churches. We shall then consider the changes of emphasis in ecclesiology which have been caused largely by ecumenical dialogue. We shall conclude with the view that all the people of God should be involved in the choice of bishops, by which we mean Christians from all the churches and confessional traditions. Because space is limited we can do no more than indicate the position briefly.

1. THE PRACTICE OF THE DIFFERENT CHRISTIAN CHURCHES IN THE CHOICE OF BISHOPS

The principle of the involvement of the whole people of God in the election of bishops, which seems to have been the general norm in the Church during its early centuries, was attacked, especially by the civil power during the so-called Constantinian period.[3] This means that it is not only the Catholic Church which needs reform in the way it chooses its bishops.

In the Christian East (although there are notable differences between one Church and another),[4] the choice of bishops and patriarchs has remained closest to the rule set down in canon 4 of the Council of Nicaea and Justinian's *Novellae* 123 and 137. This calls the bishops of the province (*eparchia*), who must be at least three, to decide by majority verdict on the new bishop from a list drawn up by the clergy and laity. The metropolitan bishop's rule is one of confirmation. In practice the laity is represented by the civil power, whose intervention is often decisive.

In the Western Church, we need to distinguish between the different confessional traditions. In the Anglican communion, at least in England, bishops are appointed by royal nomination, chosen by the Prime Minister. During the course of this century, Church officials have had a greater, though still limited say in this choice.[5] The situation is different in the Episcopalian Church in the US. Here the laity take part together with the clergy in the election of their own bishops. There are similar forms of election in Canada, Scotland and other provinces of the Anglican communion.[6]

Only some Lutheran churches (in Sweden, for example) and an even more limited number of reformed churches (the German-Swiss churches until the last century, Schaffhausen until the beginning of this century, the Danubian churches until now) have kept the episcopate (or at least an Antistes or Deacon). However, most of the Lutheran and reformed churches do not have a bishop in the Catholic sense, although we should remember that according to reformed theology, every pastor should be thought of as a bishop.[7] Authority is exercised by synods. There are also posts designated by various names (president of the synod, superintendent, moderator, etc.) who in various degrees fulfil the functions of leader and president in the church.

At any rate, election is the general criterion for choosing those who are to hold the various posts of responsibility in the church and for the synodal assemblies themselves in all the Christian communities which follow the Reformation in one way or another. In principle, the laity or representatives of the laity take part in these elections. Choice by the community by means of elections is justified on theological grounds and seems to have been the most successful way of guaranteeing the church's independence from the civil power.[8]

Other articles in this issue describe the present procedure in the Catholic Church in more detail. However, it is as well to remind ourselves here that appointment by Rome, which appears to be the general rule today, is not only a relatively recent innovation in the history of the Church, but is practised in a much less absolute manner than is generally believed. In the Eastern churches in communion with Rome, Rome merely confirms or accepts the new bishop who has been elected by the bishops of the local *eparchia*.[9] There are dioceses, especially in German-speaking countries, which have kept the right to designate or present a candidate (who is not necessarily accepted) in cathedral chapters. There is also the practice of consultation, established by the new rules of 1972[10] in the Latin Church. This practice seems to be growing in importance and frequency, especially in the young churches. All this goes to show that the way of choosing bishops varies, even within the Catholic communion. Further developments are possible without jeopardising either the Catholic conception of the role of Christ and the Spirit in the bishop's mission or the pope's Petrine prerogative.

2. LOCAL CHURCHES AND THE CHOICE OF BISHOPS IN AN ECCLESIOLOGY OF COMMUNION

Vatican II opened new ecclesiological perspectives. These have been pursued by many inter-confessional dialogues during the past few years. They have made the baptised more aware of their dignity as children of God and brothers and sisters of each other (Matt. 23:8). This has reawakened the urge to share more actively in the life of the community and not just in liturgical prayer (SC 11. 14. 19 etc.) or the apostolate (see LG 31.33; AA. 2 etc.) but also in the government of the community (see LG 12. 32. 37). The sharing of the whole people of God in the choice of their own bishops appears to be a necessary consequence of the ecclesiology of communion which is becoming more and more accepted and which has caused some ecumenically important changes of stress. We summarise these here.

*(a)  The bishop's ministry is increasingly understood as part of and related to the ministry of the whole people of God*

In the past there was a tendency to see the bishop as the one from whose fulness the other ministries descended (the juridical-christological view). Today the tendency is to see the action of God through Christ and the Spirit as primarily in the community. The whole community has a ministry, with a variety of services and functions and every Christian shares in the universal priesthood and the mission to serve the world. Every Christian has received his own charisma from the Spirit. The ministerial character of the whole community attains a kind of fulness in the ministry of president of the community whose function is to serve the unity of the baptised. This function is fulfilled for each group of Christians (the parish) by the ordained minister, and by the bishop who acts as a point of convergence for all the various charismata. The sign of ordination manifests more clearly both its origin in Christ and the priority of the divine initiative, for the sake of building up the body of Christ and faithfully proclaiming the one gospel.[11] But the rite of ordination itself, which requires the faithful to ask for or at least to agree to the ordination of their bishop, demonstrates that the episcopal ministry cannot be separated from the ministry of the whole community. It must be an expression of this ministry and take into account the people of God's supernatural discernment supported by the Spirit of truth (LG12).

*(b)  The Church is thought of increasingly from the starting point of the local church*

The choice of bishops by Rome was the result of a complicated development, which showed the prevalence within the Catholic Church of the concern to maintain communion at the level of the universal Church over the respect due to the autonomy of the local church. Today, however, there has been a rediscovery of the fact that the full presence and manifestation of the Church of Christ lies primarily in the local churches, where people hear God's word, celebrate the Eucharist, live together in faith, prayer and love, and are given the mission to serve the world. These are fully ecclesial subjects because 'in them and of them the one unique Catholic Church is constituted' (LG 23). The bishop himself is a sign of the apostolic succession by becoming bishop of a particular local church. The Church with all its activities of faith, liturgy, sacrament, ministries, remains within the apostolic succession, and this fact is recognised by the taking part of other bishops in the ordination of the local bishop. On the other hand 'absolute' ordinations, independent of a relation to a particular church, are increasingly being questioned. Now the local churches are being given back rights and powers which during the course of history had been appropriated by Rome.[12] It would seem that this process should be completed by the giving back to the local churches the power to take part in a decisive way in the choice of their own bishop.

*(c) The unity of the Church must be increasingly understood as a communion of 'sister churches' (over which Rome lovingly presides)*

The concept of unity within the Catholic Church has itself been profoundly modified in the course of the last few years. We must go beyond what was perhaps explicitly intended by Vatican II and take into account all the consequences of some of its more prophetic texts, such as UR 14-17. We must bear in mind the importance of Paul VI's achievement in relation to the Eastern churches.[13] Then we can say that the unity that should exist in the Catholic Church is that of a communion of 'sister churches', who recognise the right of the Church of Rome to 'preside in love' (Ignatius *Ad Romanos*). This service by the Church of Rome must be done 'only to sustain and not to erode the structures of the local churches'.[14] However, this ecclesiology of communion does not exclude but requires close links between the local church, the neighbouring churches (today this in fact means episcopal, regional and national conferences) and the Church of Rome. Rome's role will be increasingly recognised by all to the extent that it shows genuine respect for the autonomy of the local churches and rigorously applies the principle of help and support.[15]

In practice, in the choice of bishops, the ecclesiology of communion requires a redressing of the balance between the local and universal component of the Church. This must correct the present one-sidedness and create a system of choice in which the local community, both clergy and laity, are involved in a decisive manner. This does not mean that both episcopal conferences and Rome cannot also have a say in the choice, and thereafter the ordination of the local bishop. This would be a sign of the communion in the same apostolic faith with the whole universal Church of all time and throughout the world.

### 3. A SINGLE *EPISKOPE* FOR ALL CHRISTIANS

Although the ecumenical movement recognises the legitimacy not only of a theological pluralism but also of a pluralism in ecclesial structures, it still seems, even though we cannot foresee how it will happen, that in the future we should strive for the creation of a single *episkope*, a single common ministry for all the baptised and all Christian groups living in a single area. This perspective of a single episcopate has always been adopted by the orthodox Church, as is shown, for example, by the appeals it makes to the Latin Church, whereas the latter appointed titular bishops (*in partibus infidelium*) of sees which already had an orthodox bishop.[16] It is shown even more clearly in the Latin Church's difficulties with the uniate churches, especially the more recent ones, which were thought of more as an obstacle that as a way to unity. However, the same perspective emerges from more recent documents on the dialogue between the Anglican and the Catholic Church.[17] And in churches which properly speaking do not have an episcopate in the traditional Catholic form, there are strong tendencies in ecumenical dialogue towards considering the possibility of restoring an *episkope* as a 'sign of the continuity and unity of the Church'.[18]

Because all the baptised belong to the one Church, their communion ought to be made visible in a single ministry, with a president responsible for the communion and mission of the whole local community. This would have to be expressed by the local church itself, which would choose its president, perhaps by means of a two-tier election, through a 'conciliar' type of body on which not only both clergy and laity would be represented but also followers of the different confessional traditions existing in the local church. The participation of the bishops of the province (the episcopal conference) and of the Roman See itself, if not necessarily in the choice, at least in the ordination of the new bishop, and the receiving of him into their own communion, will still continue to be the sign of his acceptance into communion with the Catholic and Apostolic Church.[19]

*Translated by Dinah Livingstone*


## Notes

1. Groupe des Dombes *Le Ministère épiscopal. Réflexions et propositions sur le ministère de vigilance et d'unité dans l'Eglise particulière* (Taizé 1976) pp. 45-46.

2. Cajetan had good reason, in his project for reforming the Church which he drew up for Adrian VI, to propose the full restoration of the election of bishops, by secret ballot, according to conscience, to avoid corruption. He suggested this as an essential provision for purifying the Church at a time when the Protestant Reformation was beginning (see R. E. McNally 'Adrian VI and Church Reform' in *Archivum Historiae Pontificiae* 7 [1969] 277). But the proposals to give back to the people the right to elect bishops, which were put forward by a number of bishops at the Council of Trent, were not accepted because of the 'spirit of the times'. It was a period which saw the development of absolutism and was dominated by fear of the Protestants. See R. Trisco 'The Debate on the Election of Bishops in the Council of Trent' in *The Jurist* 34 (1974) 257-291.

3. The interference of the civil power in the election of bishops began in the fourth century and thereafter increased. Reaction to this interference, begun in the West from the eleventh century onwards, resulted in concentrating the choice of bishops in the hands of the clergy (cathedral chapters) and the pope. However, the civil powers continued to intervene in episcopal nominations, even in the Catholic Church. In 1832 A. Rosmini in his *Le cinque piaghe della Santa Chiesa* (new edition, Brescia 1966) called this interference one of the wounds of the Church. The pope's freedom to nominate bishops became complete at the beginning of the twentieth century. Today it is almost total except in Eastern European countries: see P. V. Aimone Braida *L'intervento dello Stato nella nomina dei vescovi con particolare riferimento ai paesi non concordatari dell'Europa occidentale* (Rome 1978). This is one of the most serious reasons given for reserving episcopal nominations to the Roman See.

4. A fairly comprehensive view is given in C. de Clercq *Fontes juridici ecclesiarum orientalium. Studium Historicum* (Rome 1967). For the Coptic patriarchate of Alexandria, see the interesting description of the selection—the election of three nominees by clergy and laity and choice of the patriarch from among these three by lot—in 'Koptische Patriarchenwahl. Eindruche eines aussenstehenden' in *Der Christliche Osten* 27 (1972) 15-22.

5. O. Chadwick 'The Anglican Practice in the Election of Bishops' in *Concilium* 7 (1972) 140-146.

6. J. L. Moreau 'Choosing Bishops in the Anglican Communion' in *The Choosing of Bishops* ed. W. W. Bassett (Hartford 1971) pp. 74-84.

7. 'Il faudra tout d'abord rappeler que l'Eglise révendique la dignité épiscopale pour tous ses pasteurs': sic J. J. von Allmenn *Le Saint Ministère selon la conviction et la volonté des Réformés du XVI siecle* (Neuchâtel 1968) p. 213. He also explains the reasons why the Reformers rejected the term bishop, which they thought too tainted, and the rapid disappearance of a hierarchy of jurisdiction which had at first been accepted. He holds that the reformed churches, although they

are sociologically considered presbyterian, should be thought of as episcopalian because every pastor is a bishop. See also H. Roux 'Le Ministère d'unite l'Eglise locale et l'episcopat en perspective reformée' in *Etudes theologiques et religieuses* 5 (1976) 39-57.

8. A. Ganoczy *Calvin et Vatican II. L'Eglise servante* (Paris 1968) p. 11. But we should rememeber the fate of the German Church under nazism.

9. M. M. Wojnar 'The participation of the Clergy and Laity in the Election of Bishops according to the discipline of the Oriental Catholic Churches' in *The Choosing of Bishops* (see note 6) pp. 61-73. The *Motuproprio Cleri Sanctitati* (AAS 49 [1957] 433-603) had restricted the autonomy of the Eastern Churches but Vatican II established that they were restored to 'the rights and privileges (of the patriachs) according to the ancient traditions of every church and the decrees of the ecumenical councils' (OE 9).

10. *Consilium pro publicis Ecclesiae negotiis, Episcopis facultas*. Normae de promovendis ad episcopale ministerium in Ecclesia latina. AAS 64 (1972) 387-391.

11. 'The laying on of hands is an efficacious sign which introduces and confirms the Christian in the ministry conferred. The ministry given does not derive from the community neither does the subject receive from the community the authority he is to exercise. He receives it from the living Christ who offers it to the community and inserts it into its life.' ('La presenza di Cristo nella chiesa e nel mondo', dialogue between World Alliance of Reformed Churches and the Secretariat for the Unity of Christians (Italian edition) (Turin 1979) n. 98.

12. *Motuproprio Pastorale Munus* of 30/11/63 in AAS 56 (1964) 5-12; *Motuproprio De Episcoporum muneribus* of 15/6/66 in AAS 58 (1966) 467-472; *Motuproprio Episcopales Potestates* of 2/5/67 in AAS 59 (1967) 385-390, etc.

13. E. Lanne 'Eglises-soeurs. Implications écclesiologiques du Tomos Agapis' in *Istina* 25 (1975) 47-74.

14. *L'autorita nella chiesa*. Document of the Anglican-Catholic commission (Venice 1976) n. 24c Cf. LG 27.

15. Principle accepted by Paul VI as the directive criterion in the relations between Rome and the local churches, for example in his speech to the Synod of Bishops of 1969 (*Documenti Cathol.* 66 [1969] 1012).

16. Practice abandoned today after the basis for the complaints of the orthodox had been recognised.

17. *L'autorita nella chiesa* (see note 14) nos. 5 and 8. See also H. J. Derek 'Church Government in England: past, present and future' in *The Clergy Review* 60 (1975) 420-428. This is an impassioned plea for the fusion of the Anglican and Catholic episcopates into a single elected episcopate, which would thus become more autonomous both from the State and from Rome.

18. *Fede e Costituzione. Documento di Accra sul Ministero* no. 37. See also 'Ministry in the Church. A Statement by the Theology Section of the Roman Catholic-Presbyterian Reformed Consultation' in *Journal of Ecumenical Studies* 9 (1972) 589-612 no. 13 e. The Dombes group in *Le ministère episcopal* (see note 1) invite the Protestants to rediscover the meaning of *episkope* and to restore it (nos. 73 and 78), with the prospect of joining in 'a single *episkope* in the one Church' (no. 77). G. F. Moede *The Office of Bishop in Methodism. Its History and Development* (Zurich 1964) invited Methodists to accept the episcopate with a view to union with the Anglican Church and episcopal churches in general.

19. We do not discuss the fact that, if a single *episkope* is not truly achieved, the way of choosing bishops in communities, which would eventually restore full communion with Rome, would remain the same as it is now. Rome would merely welcome the new bishops into communion with it (and vice versa).

# PART III

*Ecclesial Organisation*

Hartmut Zapp

# The Nomination of Bishops in accordance with Existing Law and the Draft *Liber II de Populo Dei* of 1977

IN ACCORDANCE with c. 329, art. 2 CIC the nomination of bishops is in common law a matter of free papal decision. Nevertheless, by special legal provisions, mainly of concordat law, it is to some extent associated with the electoral, presentation or advowson, and nominational rights of third parties, which are, however;.excluded from the subsequent treatment.[1] Among these specified forms of associated appointment, the code of canon law features only the right of election by a college (chapter), which is referred to expressly as a concession (cc. 329, art. 3, 321). According to the foregoing, the candidate elected is the one who has received at least the absolute majority of votes of the electoral college. Although many of the legal provisions of the CIC demonstrate the continuity of canon law with corresponding definitions of the past, this is not the case in regard to the nomination of bishops, for the free appointment of bishops by the pope is an unprecedented formulation[2]; the principle of traditional ecclesiastical electoral law, which until 1918, in spite of its erosion by papal reservation, was at least in theory general canon law, was 'turned upside-down'[3] by the CIC provision. Moreover this papal right of free appointment of bishops is 'not the outcome of one particular course of development or even of one determined mainly by ecclesiastical thinking'.[4] Since to a great extent purely ecclesiastico-political reasons have led in the course of the evolution of canon law to so strong an emphasis on the free papal right to appoint bishops as is found in the *Codex Iuris Canonici*, there are no fundamental canonistic objections to a reintroduction of the election of bishops as a matter of common law,[5] even 'the participation of the laity in such an election' is possible in principle,[6] although it is still excluded by c. 166 CIC.

At the Second Vatican Council the topic of the appointment of bishops at first received little attention and was included only subsequently in the schema for *Christus Dominus* (art. 20).[7] In the first place this scheme postulates the unrestricted freedom and independence of ecclesiastical authority in the nomination of bishops. It is especially noteworthy that initially the laity are in general accorded no form of associated right to choose, nominate, propose or suggest bishops.[8] Only after protracted interventions by several Fathers was 'laity' replaced by 'state authorities'. This alteration in the text is an explicit dissociation from the long-lasting equation in canon law of the laity with the power of the state; it also clearly shows that in regard to the appointment of bishops the Council was essentially concerned to exclude the participation of secular state authorities. Although this form of expresssion does not affirm the participation of the laity in the nomination of bishops, it no longer wholly excludes it. Hence such participation can always be introduced in the form of more explicit post-conciliar canon law, as the official explanation of the textual revision in fact stresses.[9]

As with many desires and recommendations of the Second Vatican Council, provisions were made regarding the implementation of the decree *Christus Dominus*, 20. In the *motu proprio Ecclesiae Sanctae* of 6 August 1966, I:10[10] the papal prerogative of the free nomination and appointment of bishops was emphasised but it was laid down that, annually, in accordance with provisions yet to be published, the bishops' conferences should propose candidates for the episcopate to the Holy See. This counts as the first general appearance of the nominational procedure already widespread in practice for particular areas.[11] The guidelines referred to in *Ecclesiae Sanctae*, I:10 did not appear until 1972. Before then, however, with the *motu proprio Sollicitudo omnium ecclesiarum* of 24 June 1979 on the duties of the legates and envoys of the Holy See,[12] important provisions regarding the nomination of bishops had been promulgated.

Among the *desiderata* of the Fathers at the Second Vatican Council was the restriction of the influence of apostolic delegates in favour of the primary responsibility of bishops in their own right. This request of the Council was 'used', however, 'to extend the right of apostolic delegates and to increase their power'.[13] This is especially clear in the strengthening of their position in the procedure for the selection of candidates for the episcopate. In accordance with the provisions of *Sollicitudo omnium ecclesiarum* VI, the competence of the bishops' conferences conferred through *Ecclesiae Sanctae* I:10 is largely confined to the preparation of lists of *episcopabiles*. It is accordingly the concern of the apostolic delegate—not, as one might have expected after *Ecclesiae Sanctae*, of the bishops' conference—to 'begin the usual informative process' leading to the nomination of bishops and 'to present the names of suitable candidates to the responsible curial authorities', as well as to indicate which candidate seems to him most appropriate (VI, 1). In fulfilling this duty, the pope's representative can at his own discretion consult clergy and 'prudent laymen' (VI, 2a), but in so doing must keep to the guidelines laid down by the Holy See and must finally also 'keep in mind the competence of the bishops' conference' (VI, 2b). In addition, attention must be paid to duly guaranteed privileges, properly accorded rights and any mode of procedure approved by the Holy See, which means above all any special provisions agreed with individual states (such as concordats). Clearly, in accordance with these stipulations, less significance is attached to the proposals for candidature made by a bishops' conference after collegial discussion than to the apostolic delegate's choice; one must also remember that the pope is not bound by the proposals made. It is obvious that this section of the now valid canon law regarding the nomination of bishops is wholly inappropriate to the expectation that certain norms would result from the eventual reform of the code of canon law: norms, that is, which might well restrict the prerogative of papal nomination of bishops in favour of elections by bishops' conferences, or even electoral committees with lay participation. Instead central papal power is much further extended by this law; and the free, individually responsible right of decision by bishops is limited, and the coresponsibility of clergy and laity made difficult if not impossible.[14]

In view of this key position accorded to apostolic delegates,[15] and in spite of the considerable rearrangement of the subject matter, in the end the norms for the reformulation of the selection of candidates for the episcopate in the Latin Church[16] announced in *Ecclesiae Sanctae* I:10 and promulgated on 25 March 1972 are only of secondary importance. These norms came into effect on 21 May 1972 on the basis of the decree *Episcoporum delectum* of the 'Consilium pro publicis ecclesiae negotiis'. According to the *motu proprio Regimini Ecclesiae Universae*,[17] this body is always responsible when negotiations with states are in question or papal legates and envoys implicated (art. 28, 49 par. 2). At the outset there is an express exclusion of all contrary provisions, especially the special stipulations for various nations promulgated by the Holy See. In spite of the conciliar request, in *Christus Dominus* 20, for free nomination of bishops independently of any state power, these new norms do not apply to all 'duly guaranteed or properly acquired privileges and those special procedures which are contractually agreed by the Holy See or approved by it in some other way' (art. XV); that is, they do not apply, for instance, to concordats or to the electoral rights of chapters.

In the fifteen, unsubdivided articles of the new law, detailed attention is paid to the so-called 'absolute' nomination procedure. In accordance with art. I, it is the right and duty of bishops—an innovation for the CIC—to nominate candidates for the episcopate to the Holy See. These candidates do not have to come from the bishops' own dioceses. General vicars are expressly excluded from this right of nomination. The requisite information is to be provided by the bishops in consultation with priests from the diocesan chapter, the council of priests or the diocesan or religious clergy, and even the laity. It is nevertheless emphasised that information is not to be obtained collectively, say in meetings of the abovementioned bodies, but only from individuals. This provision has been justifiably criticised and described as the Holy See's 'fear' 'of collective or collegial consultation'.

As a rule, according to art. II, the bishops' candidates should be proposed 'at their conferences', yet each individual bishop has the fundamental right to forward his proposal without any intermediary to the Holy See. It should be noted that here 'conferences' does not refer to the national bishops' conferences—that is possible only in exceptional cases and with the previous agreement of the Holy See—but to the bishops' conferences of the ecclesiastical provinces. In association with art. X (according to which the national bishops' conference cannot offer any judgment on the lists of candidates obtained in this way, but can only convey them to their president with a two-thirds majority for information and possible comment in certain regards), this stipulation confirms a clear aversion to the (too strong?) national bishops' conferences. The additional provision (art. X:2), in accordance with which the national bishops' conference can extend this power to its standing committee or to a special commission, though always under the chairmanship of its president, changes the situation not at all.

Articles III-VIII are concerned in greater detail with right of participation, chairmanship, dates and procedure.[18] The provisions of art. VI summarise the requirements of the candidates for episcopal service (in place of can. 330-331 CIC). Many of these requisite qualities are, however, not easily outlined in legal form. Art. IX provides in a short sentence that the list of candidates together with the full minutes of the conference is to be sent by the president via the apostolic delegate to the Holy See. Whether the apostolic delegate is to express his opinion thereupon is not specifically laid down, yet his entitlement to do so without any further provision is certainly derivable from the description of duties in regard to the nomination of bishops in accordance with *Sollicitudo omnium ecclesiarum* (VI, 1).

The so-called 'relative' procedure in regard to candidates (that is, the selection of candidates in the case of the actual occupation of a vacant see) is laid down in art. XI-XIII of the norms of *Episcoporum delectum*. Reference is made initially to the (absolute) lists of the episcopal conference of the ecclesiastical province, which are to be taken into consideration in such a case, but specific emphasis is also laid upon the fact that such lists do not restrict the freedom of the pope, 'who by virtue of his office always enjoys the right to choose and nominate men proposed by another side' (art. XI:2). The supervision of the procedure of examination of the candidates' suitability and worthiness (here described as 'inquisition' rather than—as hitherto conventional—

'informative process') is ascribed to the apostolic delegate. In so doing he can consult 'prudent and truly trustworthy laymen' in addition to clergy (those named are bishops, priests and religious) (art. XII). Before the actual selection of candidates (relative list), the apostolic delegate has to obtain from the leader of the diocese (e.g., the head of the chapter) a detailed report on the situation of the diocese, in addition to which he may at his discretion consult other persons—in this case even (lay) bodies (art. XIII:1). In order to produce the tripartite proposal he will, in accordance with art. XIII:2,[19] collect individually the statements of the metropolitan, of the bishops of the province to which the vacant see belongs, and of the president of the national bishops' conference, and forward them to the Holy See together with his own opinion. A possibility provided for is the consultation of individual chapter members, members of the council of priests, or members of the clergy; the laity are not cited as possible sources of opinion.

Any summary account of post-conciliar canon law on the nomination of bishops must acknowledge that the free and untrammelled papal right of nomination is the fundamental principle of these norms. The proposal lists of the bishops or bishops' conferences are—in a strict legal sense—unbinding, and the possibilities of cooperation (no right of participation) of the clergy and especially the laity are small to minimal. Therefore, as a well-known commentary on the reformulation of the selection of candidates for the episcopate in the Latin Church justifiably puts it when summarising the existing legal situation, 'it is hardly wide of the mark to say that nominations of bishops in the Latin Church remain "essentially a matter of papal secret diplomacy with a purely informal expresssion of opinion by individuals and episcopal committees" '.[20]

Since the promulgation of canon law hitherto is certainly also to be understood as a preparation for or anticipation of the final revision of the *Codex Iuris Canonici*, we can expect the draft for this new code of canon law to contain no really major alterations to the existing legal provisions for the nomination of bishops. Hence the provisions formulated in the *Schema canomum libri II de populo Dei* promulgated on 15 November 1977 offer no essential modifications of the procedure for the nomination of bishops. The first norm of the far-reaching can. 228 of the draft lays down two forms of nomination of bishops: free nomination by the pope or the papal confirmation of duly selected candidates.[21] In comparison with the CIC, the right of election is no longer described as a concession; the statement in the preparatory papers of the codex commission that free nomination is the common law form[22] for the designation of bishops has also disappeared. Free papal right of nomination is, according to the draft, on the same level with electoral right. This is certainly a welcome formulation, yet there is not the slightest reason to supposes that, in accordance with the draft, this electoral right is anything other than that given in the CIC: that is, a particular exceptional right. The stipulations also referred to in can. 228 of the draft concern the absolute procedure for listing candidates (can. 228, par. 2), whereby the bishops or (regional) bishops' conferences forward their lists of candidates annually to the Holy See. In the relative procedure (can. 228, par. 3), the (diocesan) bishops of the province in which the vacant see lies, offer a tripartite proposal, in so far as nothing else is provided for in accordance with particular special rights. If they consider it appropriate, they can consult priests and 'prudent laity' in accordance with the requirements of the diocese and the special qualities of the candidates for the episcopate. If a diocesan bishop requires an auxiliary or suffragan bishop, he must send a tripartite proposal to the Holy See—unless special law provides otherwise. If this list contains names of candidates who were not already proposed in the absolute procedure, he must also forward the opinion of the bishops of the province in question (can. 228, par. 4). Finally, in almost word-for-word reliance on *Christus Dominus* 20, it is declared that in future no rights and privileges will be accorded to state authorities to select, name, propose or nominate bishops (can. 228, par. 5).

The requirements for suitability given in c. 230 of the *schema* once again approximate in legal terms to the provisions of the CIC; as before, the final judgment of suitability is reserved to the Holy See.

Certain difficulties arise from the draft's silence on the role of the apostolic delegate in the nomination of bishops. For instance, in the case of the relative procedure for listing candidates, it is possible to detect a contradiction between can. 228, par. 3 and *Sollicitudo omnium ecclesiarum* VI, together with *Episcoporum delectum*, art. XIII. To be sure, a formulation is desirable that clearly includes the validity of the laws referred to and their stipulations on the function of the apostolic delegate. The draft merely mentions that the proposals are to be forwarded to the Holy See. Nothing is said of the key role of the delegate in this process. We cannot, however, assume that those who drew up the draft intended to exclude the cooperation of apostolic delegates from future canon law. Therefore we are hardly in error if we read can. 182:6 of the same draft[23] as affirming those rights and duties of the delegates that are set forth as norms in both the laws referred to.

The renewed understanding of the Church emanating from the Second Vatican Council, with its express teaching on the participation of all the faithful in the threefold office of Christ and the fundamental equality of all the baptised in the Church, enables us to conclude to 'the demand for the participation of the entire people of God in the occupation of ecclesiastical offices and the reintroduction of the election of bishops'.[24] But the existing norms governing the nomination of bishops and the draft of the new code of canon law are still a long way from realising those wishes.

*Translated by John Cumming*

*Notes*

1. See the relevant comments elsewhere in this issue of *Concilium*.

2. See H. Schmitz *Kleriker- und Weiherecht* (Trier 1974) (Nachkonziliare Dokumentation 38) p. 117.

3. H. Müller *Der Anteil der Laien an der Bischofswahl* (Amsterdam 1977) (Kanonistische Studien u. Texte 29) p. 233.

4. R. Kottje 'The Selections of Church Officials: Some Historical Facts and Experiences' *Concilium* 63 (1971) 117-126, at 126.

5. See J. Neumann 'Wahl und Amtszeitbegrenzung nach kanonischem Recht' *Theol. Quartalschrift* 149 (1969) 124.

6. H. Schmitz 'Plädoyer für Bischofs- und Pfarrerwahl' *Trierer Theol. Zeitschrift* 79 (1970) 232; see also on the theological aspect of the participation of the laity in the decisions of the Church, and thus also in the election of bishops, H. Küng 'Mitentscheidung der Laien in der Kirchenleitung und bei kirchlichen Wahlen' *Theol. Quartalschrift* 149 (1969) 147ff, esp. 155.

7. See, in greater detail, Müller *Anteil*, cited in note 3, pp. 225ff.

8. See *Acta Synodalia Sacrosancti Concilii Oecumenici Vaticani II*, Vol. III pars. II (Vatican 1974) p. 64.

9. See *ibid.*, Vol. III pars. VI p. 169.

11. See Mörsdorf, LThKVatKonz II p. 186.

12. AAS 64 (1972) 386-391.

13. J. Neumann 'Unitatis vincula. Zum päpstlichen Gesandtschaftswesen' *Diakonia* 1 (1970) 140; see also H. Schmitz *Motuproprio über die Legaten des römischen Papstes* (Trier 1970) (Nachkonziliare Dokumentation 21) p. 36: 'It is clear how the form of the wish expressed by the Fathers of the Council has been followed, but not the sense. For the range of duties of the delegates is more extended than restricted'.

14. See Neumann *Unitatis vincula*, article cited in note 13 at p. 141.

15. See Schmitz *Kleriker- und Weiherecht,* cited in Note 2, at p. 130.

16. AAS 64 (1972) 386-391.

17. 15 August 1967; AAS 59 (1967) 885-928.

18. See, for greater detail, U. Mosiek *Verfassungsrecht der Lateinischen Kirche* III (Freiburg im Breisgau 1978) pp. 43ff.

19. Here the reservation in favour of particular special rights is not clearly expressed.

20. Schmitz *Kleriker-und Weiherecht*, cited in note 2, at p. 131.

21. Can. 228: § 1. Episcopos libere nominat Summus Pontifex, aut legitime electos conformat'.

22. *Communicationes* 5 (1973) p. 218: 'libera nominatione a Romano Pontifice . . .: haec est forma iuris communis'.

23. Can. 182 n. 6: 'exercere facultates et explere mandata quae ipsi ab Apostolica Sede committuntur'.

24. Müller *Anteil*, cited in note 3, at p. 6; see also pp. 235ff.

Jean-Louis Harouel

# The Methods of Selecting Bishops Stipulated by Church-State Agreements in Force Today

IN THE Roman Catholic Church today, the governing principle in the selection of all types of bishop is that they shall be freely chosen by the pope, independently of any civil, political or other body. But exceptions to this rule, and modified forms of it, do still exist. Some of these exceptions and variations are grounded in legally binding agreements between the Holy See and the relevant State, which stipulate particular methods of selection. The only categories of bishop affected in this way, however, are residential bishops, prelates *nullius*, coadjutors, and bishops to the armed forces.[1]

One such type of exception is to be found where the text of the concordat lays down that vacant bishoprics shall be filled by election. In Switzerland, the Bishops of Basel and St Gallen are still elected, under concordats agreed respectively in 1828 and 1845. Their position is therefore not the same as that of Chur. Here also, election has been preserved; in this case, however, it survived because the old common law still persisted, and the Holy See accepted the custom, though in 1948 it restricted the chapter's freedom of choice to one of three candidates designated by Rome. In Basel, by contrast, the Holy See's attempt to limit the freedom of the chapter was resisted by the civil authorities, and the canons have kept their electoral rights intact. In Germany, the bishops of some dioceses are still elected as a result of concordats,[2] as is the Bishop of Salzburg, in Austria.[3] In all these areas, the Holy See retained the principle of election in order not to violate a living local tradition, but the concordats all clearly specify that the chapters may choose only from the list of three names sent by Rome.

Bavaria is in a category of its own. The 1924 concordat provides that when a bishopric falls vacant, the chapter concerned shall draw up a list of candidates to be considered by Rome; every three years, furthermore, the Bavarian hierarchy and chapters prepare and submit to Rome a list of potential bishops, and the pope is strictly obliged to make new appointments from these combined lists. But this case is unique. In every other concordat which stipulates that the local clergy shall be consulted, the Supreme Pontiff's freedom of choice in respect of the lists to be submitted to him is expressly reserved.

A second type of exception to the principle of free papal choice, deriving again from the terms of a concordat, is found where bishops are nominated by the state. Though such cases are now extremely rare, they do still occur. In Paraguay, the State exercises a right of patronage which it claims to have inherited from the Kings of Spain and has unilaterally written into its constitution; in fact this right is based merely on customary law. But in Peru, the President of the Republic has a right of patronage which is recognised by the Holy See as being truly that of the Spanish Kings.[4] In Haïti, a concordat signed in 1860 and confirmed by an accord in 1940 entitles the President of the Republic to nominate the bishops of every diocese in the country.

The one surviving remnant of the *Padroado*—the old right of patronage enjoyed by the Portuguese monarchs—need only be mentioned for its historical interest. Only one diocese, that of Macao, is now affected by it, and as the Portuguese President simply nominates whoever the Holy See suggests is the most suitable candidate, exercise of the right is now just a formality.

Since Spain renounced its prerogative in 1976, there are today only two areas of Western Europe where the State retains any rights in the nomination of bishops: the Principality of Monaco, with its individual arrangement,[6] and more particularly, Alsace and Lorraine. In the French dioceses of Strasburg and Metz, the provisions of the 1801 French concordat are still in force, and they are still being applied today when there is a vacancy to be filled. As Alsace and Lorraine belonged to Germany, not to France, from 1871 to 1918, they were not affected by the disestablishment of the French Church in 1905, and still come under the concordat. In consequence, it is the President of the French Republic who nominates their bishops, though in practice he reaches agreement with Rome before the nomination is made officially.

The various methods of selection considered so far all conflict with the principle whereby bishops are freely chosen by the pope. There is, however, another system, the *droit de regard* or right to consultation, known also as prenotification. This system leaves the pope complete freedom of choice. At the same time it, nonetheless, recognises that the appointment may be of legitimate concern to the secular authorities and offers them a means of voicing their interest. The following countries, listed in the order in which it was agreed, at present exercise this right: France, by the 1921 memorandum; Italy (1929 concordat); Austria (1933 concordat); the Federal Republic of Germany (1933 concordat) and several of the individual states with separate concordats (Bavaria, 1924; Prussia, 1929; Baden, 1923); Ecuador (1937 *modus vivendi*); Portugal (1940 concordat and missionary accord); Dominican Republic (1954 concordat); Poland (1956 decree);[7] Venezuela (1964 accord); Tunisia (1964 *modus vivendi*); probably Hungary, following the 1964 accord, the text of which has still not been made public; Argentina (1966 convention); El Salvador (1968 convention on bishops to the armed forces); Colombia (1975 concordat); Spain (1976 accord).

For the last fifty years—if we leave aside the right which Spain was granted, but has in any case now renounced—the Holy See has been very careful to allow the States with which it has made agreements no rights beyond that of consultation, the aim of this policy being to recognise the legitimate concern of the State but to preserve intact the Church's freedom in the choice of bishops.

The right of consultation effectively meets this aim because all it gives the State is the chance to raise objections against the particular candidate it is being consulted about. Since 1928, moreover, all the concordats and accords granting this right have laid down a fixed time limit, usually a month, within which the objections must be made, and have stipulated that the whole consultative process must be carried through with the utmost secrecy.

The kinds of objection allowable have also been restricted. The concordats signed since the First World War no longer mention opposition based on civil grounds, but deal solely with political objections. A further restriction, dating from the concordat of

Baden in 1932, excludes party political considerations, so that now only objections of a general political nature are permitted.

The Holy See is under no legal obligation not to proceed with an appointment to which a government is opposed. The right to consultation is not a right of veto; it entails for Rome only a moral obligation not to make an appointment in the face of a legitimate objection.[8] But this fact in no way renders it worthless from the point of view of the State, as Rome appears to have always scrupulously respected objections from governments when she thought them justified, that is, compatible with the terms of the concordat. Thus where France is concerned, it has been said that 'We are in fact quite confident that the Holy See has always respected objections from the government'.[9] So although it is only morally binding on the Holy See, the right to consultation provides governments with an effective guarantee.

A final point concerning the right to consultation: many of the countries which have agreed to it for residential and coadjutor bishops have been much more demanding when it came to the selection of chaplains to the armed forces, and the texts of a number of concordats stipulate that this category of bishop is to be chosen jointly by the State and the Holy See.[10]

We have seen that concordats and other Church-State agreements of comparable legal force lay down varying provisions about the selection of bishops. To what extent could these provisions—and indeed the agreements themselves—prove to be hindrances if a return to the practice of having bishops elected by the people were to be envisaged?

First, the few agreements still in force under which the State has the right to nominate bishops would unquestionably preclude any such move. The Second Vatican Council asked States with this prerogative to forego it of their own accord, after consultation with the Holy See.[11] Argentina, Colombia and Spain have agreed to do so. But there are some other countries which have failed to respond to the Council's request and are still exercising their right of nomination.

A second major obstacle to the change would be the agreements that stipulate election by the chapter for some bishoprics. And yet another would be the clause by which the pope is required to choose Bavarian bishops from a list drawn up by the local clergy.

Lastly, the very existence of a concordat would be an impediment. If the Holy See wished to introduce some kind of electoral system in which bishops were chosen by the clergy and laity of the diocese involved, it would only be able to do so in areas where it was itself in complete control of the selection of bishops; in other words, in areas with no Church-State agreement whatever.[12]

Even the right to consultation seems difficult to reconcile with any kind of return to episcopal elections. It might be thought that the elections could be introduced into the system as it stands, with the vote appearing simply as a first stage in the pope's decision, and the Holy See for its part agreeing to nominate the man elected and then to consult the State about him in the usual way. But under these conditions it would scarcely be possible to keep the name of the person elected a secret, and the consultation procedure would then not take place with the secrecy stipulated in the texts. Consequently, if the Holy See accepted an objection raised by the government and did not appoint the candidate who had been elected, that would be tantamount to a public rejection of the choice expressed by the clergy and faithful, and would give rise to a considerable ill-feeling.

For similar reasons, it is pointless to imagine that, were selection of bishops to be made elective, an amended version of the right to consultation, compatible with episcopal election, could ever be negotiated with states which now enjoy the right. Under an agreement so revised, if the State raised serious objections against the candidate elected, it would in effect be asking the voters to publicly disavow their own choice. Psychologically, it is impossible to expect any government to put itself in that position, unless, like the Frankish Kings, the State were entitled to confirm the election.

There are perhaps some States which would agree to give up their right to consultation if a system of episcopal election were established. But this solution could well prove to be more dangerous than any other, because it would allow governments to play a much more active role in the selection process than they can under the right of consultation. Authoritarian regimes would obviously welcome a return to the elective system. At present, however little they may like having their bishops designated from outside, by a 'foreign' power, i.e., the Holy See, they have no choice but to accept it, whereas if elections were restored, the authorities would exploit the complete control they have over the population to ensure that all the bishops were mere tools of the government. Even in democratic countries, care would be needed to ensure that the episcopal elections did not become party political, like parliamentary or local elections.

In conclusion, the Holy See has now in the main achieved the aim it has struggled after for centuries, and has effectively stripped the State of any say in the nomination of residential and coadjutor bishops. It has attained a balance between the freedom needed by the Church and the rightful concern of the State. But if an elective system in which the clergy and laity played a dominant part were reintroduced, this delicate balance between Church and State could well break down. For then, all too easily, the selection of bishops could fall prey more completely than ever before to political concerns and the power of the State.

*Translated by Ruth Murphy.*

*Notes*

1. With a few exceptions, titular bishops other than those just listed in the text are not involved in Church-State agreements. See J.-L. Harouel *Les Désignations épiscopales dans le droit contemporain* (Paris 1977).

2. Prussian concordat, 1929; Baden concordat, 1932; German concordat, 1933; accord between the Holy See and North Rhineland-Westphalia, 1956.

3. Austrian concordat, 1933.

4. Pius XI recognised that Peru has this right in the brief *Praeclara*, in 1876, following an agreement.

5. Missionary accord, 1928.

6. By virtue of the bull *Quemadmodum*, 1887, when the bishopric falls vacant the Prince of Monaco proposes three candidates to the pope.

7. This decree was the result of an understanding between the Polish government and bishops.

8. The only text which clearly states that the Holy See is legally bound to withdraw its nominee if the government raises a valid objection is the accord with Venezuela, 1964. Given the attitude of the Polish and Hungarian governments, the actual practice in those countries is closer to joint nomination than to consultation.

9. R. Metz 'Les Nominations épiscopales en France et plus spécialement dans les diocèses concordataires de Strasbourg et de Metz' *Revue de droit canonique* 8 (1958) 104.

10. The texts concerned are the German and Portuguese concordats; the 1957 accord with Argentina; the 1958 convention with Bolivia; the 1961 convention with Paraguay; the 1961 decree of the Consistorial Congregation, concerning Peru; and the 1976 accord with Spain.

11. See paragraph 20 of the Council's decree *Christus Dominus*.

12. In practice, of course, the actual obstructionism of some governments must be reckoned with. The Soviet Union is just one vast mosaic of vacant bishoprics; Czechoslovakia has now (1979) only three residential bishops for fourteen dioceses. However, these states would probably find an electoral system to their liking, since it would let them fill the ranks of the hierarchy with puppets of the regime.

Jean Rémy

# The Collaboration of
# the People of God in the Choice and
# Appointment of Bishops

CONFRONTED with a problem recognised as theologically important, the sociologian's first reaction will be to try to formulate it in appropriate sociological terms. Having done this, he hopes to help in the invention of realistic solutions which take account of the dangers to be avoided and the aims to be pursued.[1]

The discussions one sometimes hears about the *sensus fidelium* indicate either a very rudimentary knowledge of the rules of group dynamics or an uncritical acceptance of certain stereotypes propagated by liberal society. A knowledge of the rules of group dynamics seems to us essential for the devising of alternatives, and the bulk of this article will be devoted to this. We shall end with a few suggestions.

One oversimplification is to suppose that a large group functions in the same way as a small group. Small groups work by mutual acquaintance: direct personal relationships are vital in holding them together. There is a situation of relative transparency within the group. The problem to be solved is completely different when the size of the group increases. Now mediated knowledge becomes important to the integration of the group. This presupposes a process of communication in which collective symbols become increasingly important and are embodied in symbolic figures who are trusted on the basis of external criteria of credibility. Islands of mutual acquaintance may even develop, forming in the featureless sea of non-knowledge. In such a context 'non-transparency' must be a key concept in formulating modes of participation.[2] This is also the context of the idea of public opinion, which is quite different from the sum of individual reactions.[3]

Another oversimplification is to suppose that everyone can express his or her preferences in relation to their needs. The idea of clear awareness is probably connected with a rationalist and voluntarist view of human beings which does not give sufficient scope to the emotions. Even the organisers of surveys are beginning to indicate the extent to which opinion fluctuates and reacts to circumstances. Nonetheless, if the analysis is carried far enough, a degree of coherence may emerge from the fluctuations. These explanatory principles, however, are not perceived by spontaneous awareness. These in-depth studies make possible the organisation of publicity and propaganda campaigns. The importance of the unconscious, not just in individuals, but also as a collective phenomenon, thus confirms, by a different route, the need to take account of non-transparency in devising forms of participation. Moreover, on many issues there may well be a large number of 'don't knows'. To establish realistic procedures for participation we must be wary of any populist assumptions.

Another factor is that liberal society is based on the fiction of the average individual and global decisions, to be taken on the basis of a totalling of individual reactions. The principle of the majority makes it possible to produce socially legitimate decisions. In fact, however, the life of a society does not exist and develop in function of a totality of individual decisions as if group phenomena did not exist and were not fundamental to individual identities. In this connection analysts of public opinion are very worried about integrating minority phenomena, since these indicate tendencies which may very well be a majority in the future, even if their expressions then are very different from their present initial forms. The ideal of social movement enables us to understand the way in which new collective priorities form. This social movement itself operates only in so far as it brings about a new attitude to guilt, for example, pride in not feeling guilt according to the accepted norms, creating doubt in society as a whole, creating a new unity with regard to common values.[4] All this presupposes that we distance ourselves from the immediate and reintroduce a temporal and collective dimension. Instead of starting from the implicit assumption of the stereotypes propagated by liberal society in which the individual is central to meaning, we need to be able to relocate the vocation of the individual within a collective history the meaning of which begins before the individual and ends after him or her.

The social movement, with its ability to question and rethink, leads us to pick out another problem, disagreements, which may or may not be expressed in conflicting behaviour.[5] We cannot assume, as populist views often do, that if the mass of the people become articulate the result will be consensus. How are we to cope with this situation of disagreement? Are we to use the technique of a mother who prevents conflicts from being expressed, when this may sometimes lead to the avoidance of important subjects and reduce discussions to trivialities? If these conflicts have to be accepted, this cannot be done in the same way in groups which can operate by means of a continuing and explicit negotiation of priorities and in groups where views are based on membership of a common world.[6] This may be one difference between the worlds of economics and politics and that of religion. The particular procedures valid for the former are not immediately transferable to the latter. The distinction between 'ground' and 'figure' formulated by Gestalt theories in the psychology of perception is very important to an understanding of the structuring of meaning in both cases. In the former the expression of differences, even of oppositions, takes shape against a background of affirmation of the common identity. Starting from this, the members must then discuss the origin of the tensions and conflicts. In Church circles one is often more aware of the conflict between the local and the general than of the conflicts within the local church which may result in solidarities and oppositions which go beyond the boundaries of the local church.

While it may take on a particular connotation in the Church, the opposition between the local and the global, between the periphery and the centre, is one which has to be faced generally in society. The person involved in the local situation has a better knowledge of the context, which enables him to have a unified view. He is thus much closer to the existential. The person who takes the global view is certainly at a distance from everyday life, but he has access to comparative data which enable him to indicate dangers and to coordinate. All social life is pulled in this way between centrifugal forces and centripetal forces. The centrifugal person is in danger of becoming totally absorbed in local problems, while the centripetal one may become trapped in the abstract affirmation of principle and codification.

Cutting across this tension there is another which has a different source and is acquiring increased importance in present-day society as compared with what it had in previous centuries, which were dominated by the growth of nationalism and the break-up of Christianity.

The result is that the individual may define his or her identity by means of multiple affiliations not based on demarcations of the same territory. In some ways this makes possible a deterritorialisation of solidarities and conflicts. In such a social context individuals and groups may develop partial solidarity with the Church and, in addition, aspirations with regard to the Church which are not in accord with those of other social groups. In this connection, what do we think of the pastoral council at which, instead of gathering Christians without any other social identity, apart from perhaps grouping them according to the geographical areas of the diocese, the organisers set up delegations coming from different social backgrounds, different age groups, etc? The aim of this structure was to give each group an equal chance of expressing its point of view, with the idea that the confrontation of viewpoints would gradually produce an overall position.

This process of participation is, it will be seen, complex and may go wrong if it is reduced to a simple formula, particularly since it is also necessary to allow for the importance of informal groups alongside organised structures.[7] The relationship is not as simple or direct as it appears in the political ideology of a liberal society in which, in a sense, the organisational structures are the transparent expression of a social body and provide it with an instrument of unity and action. It is necessary to have ways of relating to the structures which allow, not only for identification, but also for distance. Any social dynamic presupposes the establishment of a relationship of distance and proximity between the particular social unit and the social units of which it forms a part. Popular religion, for example, among some groups, makes it possible to have a link with the clergy and at the same time a distance from them. This distance allows for the collective expression of demands and lack of agreement with the model of religion officially proposed by the clergy, but it does not lead to a break because the fundamental role of the clergy is not questioned. The result is a permanent collective transaction which controls the relationship between the two without at first giving rise to specific organisational structures to resolve the disagreement. The organised structures, if they come into being, take shape against a background of cultural movement in which expressions of piety are at the heart of the meaning produced.

This brings us to another question about the social action which is at the heart of the ecclesial bond. This is to determine the importance of forms of leadership and areas of initiative in the Church.[8] Mutual social recognition is the result of the sharing of common symbolic actions or adherence to a common ethic or participation in common collective projects. According to the priority given to one or other, the clergy initiative which provokes adherence will be different because this influences the sorts of leadership and the types of initiative sought.[9] This may combine with the significance attributed to the organisational structures of the Church. Some people will want the clergy to be, above all, the expression of the public, official word, while others will want the clergy to give more publicity to the feelings of certain groups among the people of God. If we want to get away from theological language, it is very important to use neutral terms like 'form of leadership' rather than 'new ministries', 'priesthood', etc., though these can be brought back later.

Another factor is that changes in forms of leadership cannot be brought about by decree. They take their place in the movement of collective symbols. This movement transforms the content of what is 'believable'. For example, in Western countries many Christians can no longer believe that it is necessary to have all the children God sends. Instead they associate human dignity with the fulfilment of personal goals. This transformation of 'beliefs' in this area has not been the object of conscious individual decisions, but is a part of the evolution of collective symbols.[10] One development which makes it all the more important to mention this problem is that for some years there has been a growing questioning of the symbolic exaltation of rationality as the sovereign means of control. This questioning affects minorities, but they are sufficiently active to formulate problems which emerge into public opinion. Instead of associating the development of the reasonable with the increase in techniques for rational control, these tendencies reassert the importance of what is outside our control and so, in this sense, non-rational, in the creation of a genuinely human and therefore rational world.[11] Christians who belong to this tendency are likely to criticise the generation of those who went through the Council and call them rationalists. Seminary rectors are likely to find themselves at a loss in the face of the demands of young seminarians who are bringing the affective dimension more into the expression of their religion. We are probably emerging from a period which asserted human dignity by asserting technical and rational issues to the exclusion of affectivity, which was seen as irrational and so judged to be contrary to reason. We are probably entering another period which will devise a new synthesis between what is socially controllable and what is not controllable. This will shift social issues to some extent. At the break we have reached, we cannot imagine the next twenty years as a simple continuation and extrapolation of the issues and aspirations of the last twenty.

This change will have an effect on the internal life of the Church and especially on the more or less latent conflicts between a hierarchical model and an egalitarian model. It is likely that attempts will be made to find an area of transaction between the two rather than accept them as mutually exclusive, which gives added relevance to our subject, the local Church and the selection of bishops.

When one is faced with two mutually exclusive models one can describe the cultural universe which organises the likely features of the two tendencies in terms of the following associations and oppositions.[12]

The hierarchical model is built around the opposition base: top. The base is life; the top is competence. The top without the base is like a blind person without a guide, and it is true that competence does not consist simply of skills which can be taught and acquired by anyone. The egalitarian model is built around the opposition between sovereign individuals and the services necessary for keeping life going. Without communal services, individuals have no voices, no representatives. Nor do services have any point unless they are controlled by individuals. Individuals belong to the private sphere and so have a right to a degree of secrecy which cannot be investigated by the authorities. The authorities, on the other hand, belong to the public sphere and have no right of secrecy. This model presupposes that society is truly human when control and rationality are dispersed.

When they are followed in this way the two models are in a relation of incompatibility and are mutually corrosive. The discovery of new solutions is likely to be faster to the extent that attempts are made in society to reach a compromise between the two, particularly by questioning the primacy of either the rational or the non-rational (not to be confused with the irrational). At this point there is an attempt to bring together mastery and mystery. If this change of attitude takes place, we may suppose that in the next few years the people most highly regarded in the Church will be those who knew the old system from within and have taken an active part in the post-conciliar renewal. Their twofold experience will probably make them mediating agents capable of new syntheses.[13]

The preceding notes were an attempt to offer some guidelines as a way of avoiding the disappointments which will inevitably result from the use of over-simple images. On the basis of these, we should like to put forward some suggestions to help in devising alternatives.

1. It is important not to confuse a survey of opinion with a referendum or, worse, with a deep analysis of the movements affecting a society. These confusions are all the more pernicious because they reinforce the false idea that the most frequent attitude is the basis for determining a normal attitude. If the sociologist is interested in analysing how to evaluate attitudes regarded as legitimate, he does not make the frequency of the attitude a principal indicator of legitimacy.

2. The workings of a community cannot be transformed by decree. It is not enough to work out rational procedures; they will not create participation by themselves. This is all the more important because what is happening is not the appointment of a technical leader. No, working out procedures must be the starting-point for stimulating an effective process of mutual recognition. If one is unwilling to initiate such a process, it is better to keep to secret or private consultations to provide material for a central decision.

3. The appointment of a bishop can be an event which initiates a continuing process of mutual recognition. This presupposes that the choice is organised as a collective public event, with a period of preparation (before) and a continuation afterwards. The preparation, an important moment for heightening collective awareness, should not take place in a secular framework, as though a political or trade union leader were being appointed. The process of heightening awareness must take place in a religious setting in which a sense of mystery is stimulated by prayer and various other methods of putting worldly considerations on one side—not excluding traditional forms of abstinence. Against the background formed by this religious setting, every form of grouping and informative process should operate, not excluding the methodological contribution which might be provided by psychology and sociology: *fides quaerens intellectum*. What should be avoided is the opposite process, in which, after an analysis in human terms, people ask what faith has to add. Whatever happens, the event should be a high point initiating a different way of being together.

4. It is also important, especially in the preparatory period, to devise consciousness-raising strategies. It must be made clear that the process is based on participation. Here, there are many ambiguities to be avoided. Unfounded hopes subsequently disappointed are inevitably disheartening. Have we not seen this often in connection with pastoral councils?

5. Before discussing individuals, the group must make explicit its hopes or aspirations with regard to the future bishop. What are the priorities for the future of the community? For example,

—should the bishop gather everyone into one flock which goes forward at the same speed, holding some back and pushing others forward, or, alternatively, should he allow diversity to be expressed, even if the result is to increase tension?

—should he involve himself with the activists and their problems about commitment, leaving the mass of Christians more or less bewildered?

6. If there is a genuine political will to initiate the movement, it will be necessary to work out active strategies enabling each social group to have an equal possibility of expressing its priorities and its aspirations. This is likely to lead to more or less serious difference or oppositions, which will have to be accepted in faith. Techniques deriving from psychology and sociology will be needed at this point to depersonalise the oppositions as far as possible. A difference or a conflict does not originate first in a breakdown of affective relations. On the contrary, we have to learn to disagree while maintaining an affectively positive relationship. This is the difference which some sociologists are trying to establish between a social relation and human relations. However, this is not possible without affective maturity, which does not make fusion a condition of exchange. It is

useful to return to the distinction between figure and ground. The Church cannot function in the same way as the economic sphere, where oppositions constitute the background against which areas of consensus take shape.

7. After the appointment of the bishop the problem of the dynamics of the community will have to be faced anew, especially if there has been conflict. At this point new procedures of arbitration and innovation will have to be introduced via the bishop, but all of them must be set against a background of mystery, making the ceremony of consecration a process of emotional involvement which produces new legitimacies. The religious dimension must constantly interlock with the profane dimension and form the background against which the latter takes on form and meaning.

*Translated by Francis McDonagh*

*Notes*

1. We have taken a deliberate decision to include in these notes only our own writings or those of members of our research group. The purpose of these references is to help those interested to find further discussion of the problems analysed very briefly in these pages. These texts have been reprinted and reorganised in a more general sociological perspective in: J. Remy, L. Voyé, E. Servais *Produire ou reproduire. Pour une sociologie de la vie quotidienne, Conflits et transaction sociale* I, *Transaction sociale et dynamique culturelle* II (Brussels 1978-80).

2. 'The Diffusion of Information in the Church: a Way Out of the Unequal Dialogue' *Concilium* 63 (1971) 108-116.

3. 'Opinion publique, groupes de pression et autorité constituée dans la vie de l'Eglise catholique' *Social Compass* 19 (1972) 155-184.

4. 'La faute et la culpabilité dans la perspective de l'analyse sociologique' *Concilium* (January 1971) 1, 11-23 (with L. Voyé, F. Hambye and E. Servais); 'Innovation and the development of structures: problems posed by institutionalisation' *Lumen Vitae* 24 (English edition) (1969) no. 3 377-404.

5. 'Conflicts and sociological dynamics: questions relating to the life of the Church' *Lumen Vitae* 24 (English edition) (1969) no. 2 212-236; *Communade crista en meio urbana* (with F. Houtart; Portuguese translation of a previous work) (Lisbon 1969); 'Crise de la communauté: situation provisoire ou changement culturel?' (with F. Hambye) *Lumière et Vie* 18 (1969) no. 93 85-112; *Chiesa e società in evoluzione* (with F. Houtart) (Bologna 1974).

6. 'Eglise et partis. Le champ religieux peut-il s'organiser à la manière du champ politique?' (with L. Voyé) *Lumen Vitae* 28 (1973) no. 4 609-616.

7. *Communauté, conflit, innovation. Foi et société, Acta Congressus Internationalis Theologiae Lovaniensis* (1976) no. 5-6.

8. 'Lar religion dans une société pluraliste: jalons pour une observation du phénomène' *Social Compass* (Louvain 1966) no. 5-6.

9. 'Formele en andere machtstructure' *De Maand* (1969) no. 7 410-412; 'Les groupes informels dans l'Eglise, Ile Colloque du CERDIC, Strasbourg, mai 1971' *Sociologie des groupes informels* 11-36.

10. 'Analyse du rôle du prêtre comme indicateur privilégié des modes d'insertion de l'institution religieuse dans une société urbaine et industrielle' *Actes de la Conférence Internationale de Sociologie Religieuse* (Montreal, n.d.) 431-461; 'Aspects sociologiques d'une recherche sur les ministères dans l'Eglise' *Les Ministères dans l'Eglise de demain* (Centre Pastoral des Vocations du diocèse de Tournai 1973) (with L. Voyé) 21-50.

11. 'Communauté et assemblée liturgique dans une vie sociale en voie d'urbanisation' *Maison-Dieu,* special issue: 'Sciences Humaines et Liturgie; 'Formes liturgiques et symboliques sociales' (with J. P. Hiernaux and E. Servais) *Social Compass* (1976) 175-192; 'Le phénomène paroissial aujourd'hui. Eléments pour une interrogation sociologique' (with J. Hiernaux and E. Servais) 123 *Lumière et Vie* 25-36; 'Formes religieuses en transformation, Rapport à l'ordre social et aux structures symboliques' (with J. P. Hiernaux and E. Servais) *Actes de la 13e Conférence Internationale de Sociologie religieuse* (Lille, Editions du CISR 1975) 89-110.

12. 'Désacralisation et insertion culturelle de l'Eglise' *Economie et Humanisme* 196 (Nov.-Dec. 1970) 4-10.

13. 'Modèle hiérarchique et types de société' *Le Supplément* 123 (Nov. 1977) 459-464; 'Clandestinité et illégitimité: les fonctions de l'occulte et du mystéreiux dans la société contemporaine' (with E. Servais) *Concilium* 81, January 1973 69-80; 'Authority in the Church and socio-cultural change' *Convergence* Special issue on the crisis of authority in the Church 5 (1969) 14-18.

14. 'Point de vue sur l'année sainte comme année de réconciliation—un sociologue' *Une année Sainte pour notre temps* (Ed. du Chalet, 1974) pp. 73-79.

F

# PART IV

*Bulletins*

Lamberto de Echeverría

# The Appointment of Bishops in Spain since Vatican II

## 1. THE SITUATION AT THE TIME OF THE COUNCIL

AFTER a protracted and complicated series of negotiations,[1] an agreement with the Holy See was signed on 7 June 1941 and this was subsequently ratified in Article VII of the 1953 Concordat. This Agreement reflected the difficulties involved in its negotiation, with a complicated formula, full of subordinate clauses, which in effect produced a veto system: the Spanish Head of State could not under any circumstances cause a particular appointment to be made, since the names from which he had to choose were submitted by Rome, but he could systematically block a particular nominee, simply by always choosing a different name from the minimum of three submitted.

This veto formed the juridical basis of the Agreement, though in practice the system was less rigid, with an initial list of six names being chosen by common agreement between the Nunciature and the Ministry of Foreign Affairs, and the possibility of adding fresh names, plus the obvious fact that such an intricate process allowed for friendly mutual suggestions going beyond the strictly juridical framework. The system was a real breakthrough, since the Holy See had been fighting for years to regain its freedom to nominate bishops in Spain.[2]

In no. 20 of its Decree *Christus Dominus,* Vatican II declared that 'the right of nominating and appointing bishops belongs properly, peculiarly and of itself exclusively to the competent ecclesiastical authority', and consequently addressed itself to those authorities who retained some right in the matter, asking them with due courtesy to 'spontaneously renounce, after consultation with the Holy See, the aforementioned rights and privileges which they have, through agreement or custom, enjoyed till now'. Though this paragraph was couched in general terms, there were those who thought it was aimed particularly at the Spanish situation.[3] In fact the declaration made a great impact in Spain, and the privilege, already unpopular in many circles, began to assume the dimensions of a considerable embarrassment. Pope Paul VI approached the Spanish Head of State asking him to accede to the Council's request, and Franco replied that he was willing to do so provided this was done in the context of an overall revision of the Concordat. Negotiations for this revision were protracted, to the extent that they were unfinished at the time of General Franco's death.

## 2. THE TREATY OF 1976

The unpopularity of the privilege, confirmed by surveys and press campaigns, determined that when the regime changed, two points, the nomination of bishops and the special privileges enjoyed by the clergy, were to be decided by special treaty in advance of the negotiations for the revision of the Concordat. When the King summoned Suárez to be president of the Council of Ministers, renunciation of the privilege of presentation of names was played as a political trump card by the new government. In fact it was not long (13 July 1976) before the King, having consulted the government and the Council of the Realm, wrote to the pope saying that he 'would pose no obstacle to the renunciation of the right of presentation long associated with the Crown of Spain'. Negotiations were speedy and the new Treaty was signed on 28 July, formally ratified by both sides on 20 August and officially promulgated on 24 September. After a long, dense preamble of considerable doctrinal importance, the new Treaty established a new system for episcopal nominations.[4] This was the first of five specific agreements that were to take the place of the 1953 Concordat.

In the new Treaty, the 'nomination of archbishops and bishops belongs exclusively to the competence of the Holy See', but in the case of 'residential archbishops and bishops and coadjutors with right of succession' a special process is to be followed. Unlike the 1941 Treaty, there is no mention of permanent apostolic administrators, since these had disappeared, nor of auxiliary bishops, who had been the object of sharp controversy in the last years of the Franco regime.

A right of 'pre-notification', giving the possibility of objections on political grounds, was granted. This meant that the Spanish process of nominating bishops joined the long line of concessions of this type made by the Holy See from the Concordat with Guatemala in 1884 to those recently concluded with Argentina and Colombia.

This pre-notification gave the Spanish State the possibility of objecting on grounds of a 'general political nature', but these had to to beyond civil objections and were required to be specific, excluding vague accusations with no definite foundation. To avoid the confusion to which similar rights had led in other countries, the Spanish Treaty laid down that objections were subject to 'the prudent evaluation of the Holy See'. The time allowed for this was particularly short, since in place of the month generally allowed—and the possibility of this being extended in the case of Venezuela—a limit of a fortnight was set.

There is the usual reference to the secrecy to be observed by both parties with regard to the inquiries made prior to nomination, which corresponds to a desire of the Holy See, expressed in the new norms of 1972,[5] by which collective consultations were excluded, since 'the Holy See will avoid any form of consultation that could take on the appearance of an election'.[6]

There was one significant omission. Although the 1941 Agreement did not specify it, subsequent lengthy and difficult negotiations produced an exchange of notes on 1 February 1943 by which bishops had to swear an oath in the presence of the Head of State before taking possession of their dioceses.[7] The new Agreement was silent on this point, and the taking of the oath would seem to have passed into the realm of history.

For the appointment of the Vicar General of the Forces, who occupies a very special place in the structure of the State, a 'proposal of a *terna* of names' was foreseen, the names to be agreed between the Nunciature and the Ministry of Foreign Affairs and submitted for the approval of the Holy See. Within a fortnight, the King would put forward one of the names for nomination by the Roman Pontiff. Nothing is said about the Prelate of Ciudad Real, who therefore comes under the usual procedure, but there are well-founded rumours of the existence of a secret clause submitting the nomination of the Bishop of Seo de Urgel, by virtue of his singular political position as Prince of Andorra, to a procedure similar to that of the Vicar General of the Forces.

### 3. APPLICATION OF THE TREATY

Between the time the Treaty came into force and the present day, its application has taken place in twenty-nine nominations. The first aspect that comes to mind is that nothing has been gained by way of speed. Everyone, including the present author, saw the 1941 Agreement as a brake that would slow down the speed of nominations. Surprisingly, now that the Holy See has a free hand, and only a fortnight is allowed to lodge political objections, it has not managed to speed up its nominations. The strangest case to date has been that of the diocese of Vitoria, whose bishop's resignation was accepted on 10 July 1978, when he was retained as apostolic administrator, despite having resigned on grounds of health, without a successor being appointed until 17 February 1979, seven months later. In passing, it is worth noting that the new system makes it much easier for bishops to resign without having reached retirement age. Before, the Holy See used to resist this for fear of producing a *sede vacante* which could prove difficult to fill.

The most obvious change brought about by the new ruling is in the situation of auxiliary bishops. In order to take advantage of the one chink of freedom left in the 1941 Agreement, and in order to influence their subsequent promotion to residential sees, the Holy See nominated a whole host of auxiliary bishops during the Franco era. The situation now is that during the period between 1976 and the beginning of 1980, only two auxiliary bishops (for Bilbao and Santander) have been nominated. These both date from the first months of the Treaty, being made on 17 September 1976, which means that their nomination was quite possibly foreseen before the Treaty came into force. In a country with twenty-nine episcopal nominations since the new Treaty, there have been only seven consecrations, with ten nominations going to auxiliary bishops being given residential appointments or changing jobs.[8]

This promotion of auxiliary bishops to residential sees has broken new ground, involving a break with a previously unbroken tradition by which an auxiliary bishop was never promoted to the see of the bishop to whom he had been auxiliary.[9] The promotion of auxiliary bishops to national posts was ratified, leaving them attached to their former dioceses in a purely formal fashion,[10] and a result of these national appointments is the new case of a bishop going direct from auxiliary to metropolitan, doubtless as a result of more weight being given to his effectiveness as secretary to the Episcopate than to his formal condition of auxiliary to another metropolitan.

Although there have been significant exceptions, there has been a marked overall tendency to regionalisation, with designated bishops coming from the same region in which they are to exercise their ministry. Spain is going through a period of hectic activity on the question of regional autonomy, and this is one more example of the phenomenon, which has been marked by some extremely sharp protest movements. For many, this marks an unfortunate process of impoverishment. For the moment, however, in view of the political trauma through which Spain is passing, it would seem to be the only practicable course.

With regard to criteria for selecting candidates: these would not seem to have changed much from those previously in operation. The general opinion is that most of those nominated, nearly all of them in fact, could have been so under the old system.

*Translated by Paul Burns*

*Notes*

1. A. Marquina 'El primer acuerdo del nuevo Estado español y la Santa Sede' *Razón y Fe* (1978) 132-149, shows how far the Agreement was, contrary to the general view, a success for the Holy See. The text of the Agreement is in AAS 33 (1941) 480-481.

2. See two articles of mine on the subject: 'Renuncia a privilegios' *Iglesia y comunidad política* (Salamanca 1974) 187-208; 'La recíproca renuncia de la Iglesia y el Estado de los privilegios de Fuero y presentacíon de los obispos' *Estudios eclesiásticos* 52 (1977) 197-221.

3. 'Un tel privilège subsiste donc dans un certain nombre de pays *a commencer par l'Espagne dont le cas a probablement motivé l'intervention* du noo 20 du décret' (my italics): J.-L. Harouel in *Les Désignations épiscopales dans le droit contemporain* (Paris 1977).

4. The text of the Treaty is in AAS 68 (1976) pp. 509-512. I have commented on it in 'El convenio español sobre nombramiento de obispos y privilegio del fuero' *Rev. esp. de Der. can.* 33 (1977) 89-140.

5. *Acta Consilii pro publicis ecclesiae negotiis* 'De promovendis ad episcopatum in Ecclesia latina' in AAS 64 (1972 pp. 386-391. T. G. Barberena 'Neuvas normas sobre nombramiento de obispos' *Rev. esp. de Der. can.* 28 (1972) 657-682.

6. Harouel refers in the article cited in note 3 to the cases of Haarlem, Bois-le-Duc, Cleveland, Breda, Montreal and New York. The only case in Spain, to my knowledge, was in 1972 when the presbyteral council of San Sebastián presented a *terna*, decided on by vote, for the nomination of an auxiliary bishop, and the Holy See chose the first name on the *terna*, Fr José-Maria Setién.

7. I first published news of the exchange of notes and the swearing of the oath in my article 'El Convenio español . . .' (note 4 *supra*), in which I pointed out that the unpopularity of the oath meant that only a *presentation* of the new bishop to the Head of State was ever mentioned, with no talk of a nomination, and no pictures of the occasion on television, which was then full of reports of similar ceremonies. See pp. 121-122.

8. What O. González de Cardedal wrote in 1973 has clearly come about: 'In the long run the nomination of so many auxiliaries has till now meant an enrichment of the Spanish Church. . . . If one counts the number of auxiliaries now in existence, it is not difficult to see that all the Spanish provinces are already spoken for.' By 'changing jobs' I am referring to the auxiliary Bishop of Barcelona who in July 1979 was appointed National Director of Pontifical Missions, resident in Madrid, but still theoretically continuing as auxiliary of Barcelona. His predecessor in the post was in the same situation, as titular auxiliary of Pamplona, carrying on the practice of auxiliaries remaining in their diocese, as auxiliaries to the successor appointed on the death or resignation of the bishop to whom they were appointed auxiliary in the first place.

Following the strange course of nominations in Spain, this is what happened on 26 January this year: While the dioceses of Badajoz (vacant for a year) and Lugo (three months: both resignations that had long been foreseen), an auxiliary was named to the Archbishop of Oviedo, who is 54 years old, in a diocese with no long tradition of auxiliaries, since it has only had one in the last few years, and that very nominally since the previous one was appointed Secretary to the Episcopal Conference. . . .

9. This happened on 23 September 1978, when the auxiliary of Murcia was made diocesan. One has the impression this was done to make the promotion of the auxiliary of San Sebastián to diocesan, a little later, in November, less noticeable, and that once this had been achieved, there would be a reversal to the previous practice.

10. The post of Secretary to the Episcopal Conference, previously held by an auxiliary of Madrid, then of Oviedo, is now held by a priest, not a bishop. But an auxiliary bishop is still National Director of Pontifical Missions (note 8). Other auxiliaries have national posts as presidents of episcopal commissions, but as these do not require residence in Madrid they do not pose problems different from when these posts are held by diocesan bishops.

John Tracy Ellis

# The Appointment of Bishops and the Selection of Candidates in the United States since Vatican II

'WE, FOR the first time only . . . permitted the said priests to elect and to present to this apostolic See.'[1] Such were the words used by Pius VI in the bull of 6 November 1789, that designated John Carroll to be Bishop of Baltimore, the first episcopal appointment in the United States. Actually, the priests voted twice more in selective Carroll's two coadjutor bishops, but after 1795 the practice lapsed for almost a century until 1885 when the diocesan consultors and irremovable pastors were given the right to present a *terna* for a vacant diocese, a right that was cancelled by Rome in 1916. From the time of Carroll's election to Vatican II the methods and procedures of selecting American bishops were changed repeatedly with the widest variety of approach employed from that of the priests' vote mentioned above to the appointment by the Holy See—with no consultation with the American hierarchy—of the two Irish-born Dominicans, resident in Rome, who were named as the first and second Bishop of New York in 1808 and 1814.

Every country has its own laws and customs amid which, historically speaking, the nomination of bishops has been exercised. Thus by reason of the constitutional separation of Church and State in the United States, the nomination process has been free of the interference of government that has characterised the selection of bishops elsewhere. Carroll learned this in 1806 when his inquiry of President Jefferson concerning ecclesiastical appointments in Louisiana brought the reply that 'the scrupulous policy of the Constitution in guarding against a political interference with religious affairs[2] dictated an attitude of silence on the part of government.

If the American Church has escaped 'political interference', in the selection of bishops, it has experienced another kind of difficulty of which other countries have been relatively free. This is the rivalry and controversy that have arisen from the clash of racial and ethnic groups within the Catholic community. As early as 1833 there was deep feeling on the part of some against the Irish when, e.g., the English-born Archbishop of Baltimore, James Whitfield, remarked, 'I am sorry that any more Irish bishops are added to our hierarchy, as I fear their increase in number will have power to have others of their countrymen nominated hereafter. . . .'[3]

By reason of the extraordinary mixture of ethnic and racial elements that has marked the American Catholic community, for nigh to two centuries recurring strains of this kind have been felt in the choice of bishops. It has been an increasingly troublesome factor since Vatican II, at times acutely so among black Catholics and those of Hispanic background. The demand for representation in the hierarchy has steadily mounted among the blacks, a body of close to one million Catholics of the approximately 25,000,000 black Americans. In the present (1979) hierarchy of c. 350 members there is one black ordinary and four black auxiliary bishops. Almost certainly the pressure for more black bishops will increase, especially in dioceses with large black Catholic populations such as Chicago and Washington, and those in the State of Louisiana.

Perhaps even more insistent on greater representation have been the Catholics of Hispanic ancestry, the most rapidly growing element in the Catholic community, numbering, it has been estimated, close to one-quarter of the approximately 50,000,000 Catholics of the United States. While those of Hispanic blood are not confined to any one geographical region, they are especially numerous and articulate in the South-West and in California. Thus disappointment was expressed in 1978 in the choice for the new diocese of San Bernardino, California, just as they were gratified by the selection of two of their number as Archbishop of Santa Fe, New Mexico (1974) and Archbishop of San Antonio, Texas (1979). At present there are three ordinaries and four auxiliary bishops of Hispanic ancestry. The problem is rendered more complex by the differences within this group, i.e., between Mexicans, Puerto Ricans, and Cubans. Here, then, is a situation to which those responsible for selecting bishops for the American episcopacy will have to give increased attention. A further factor that should be kept in mind is the sheer size of the American Church. The country's 170 dioceses make the task of selection a far more exacting undertaking than is true in most countries with less than half that number of jurisdictions inhabited by a much more homogeneous Catholic population.

As Vatican II touched every phase of ecclesial experience, so did it afford fresh impetus in the question of selecting bishops, and that by reason of the Council's emphasis on expanding the process of consultation to embrace not only the clergy but the religious and the laity as well. If this trend was a healthy move away from the excessive centralisation of authority at Rome, it was not something altogether new. A broad consultation had been a feature of the early Church, which won the encouragement of Pope Saint Leo I *et al.*, who thereby sought to make real what Saint Ambrose had in mind when he remarked, 'It is normal that anyone who wishes to be believed should establish his credentials'.[4]

In an attempt to carry out Vatican II's intent various groups in the American Church have been active in the matter of selecting candidates for the episcopacy. Among them have been since 1973 the standing committee of the National Conference of Catholic Bishops, the National Federation of Priests' Councils whose task force for that purpose was formed in 1974, and the pastoral councils of certain dioceses that have participated in the process. The most active of all these groups, however, has been the Canon Law Society of America. Limitation of space makes it necessary to confine what follows largely to the CLSA's efforts on behalf of the selecting process, an undertaking that began in the late 1960s and that had as one of its earliest results the publication of a series of essays on the subject.[5]

Once the Council for the Public Affairs of the Church had issued (in March 1972) its norms for the selecting of bishops of the Latin Rite, of course, that became the official procedure for all concerned. With that in mind in 1973 the CLSA committee drew up suggestions for the implementation of the papal norms which, in turn, formed the basis of a discussion by the NCCB's committee and the CLSA. In 1976 the CLSA initiated further steps with a reactivated committee that drafted (in October 1977) a document entitled 'A Four-Phase Process for Diocesan Participation in the Process of Selecting Bishops for United States Latin Rite Dioceses'. By reason of the four-phase plan providing for collective consultation on the selection of candidates and other features, both the Apostolic Delegation and the NCCB found the CLSA's draft at variance with the papal norms and objected to it. At present the CLSA committee is reviewing the matter in light of the objections raised to their four-phase plan, and they will report again later in 1980. Parenthetically, here 'Latin' should be noted, for the eight dioceses of various Eastern Rites with nearly 600,000 members in the United States, follow other procedures which might, indeed, offer valuable alternatives more in tune with general American experience than those of the Latin Rite.

Since 1965, as before, no single approach to the selection of American bishops has given complete satisfaction. If the confidential letters of bishops seeking data on candidates have been thought by some among the least effective forms of communication, consultation with priests, religious and the laity has likewise revealed inadequacies. Such was the case in the diocese of Manchester, New Hampshire, in 1967 where not only absence of knowledge and experience inhibited the priests but, too, a measure of indifference was evident,[6] and Manchester has not been unique in this regard. When in the late 1970s the CLSA committee undertook a survey in various dioceses it became evident that much depended on the ordinary's reaction. Thus in the Diocese of Belleville, Illinois, the CLSA proposal was followed with a wide consulting process, and the appointment of William M. Cosgrove in August 1976 was seen as a welcome result of the procedure. On the other hand, in a diocese of the Pacific Coast, the bishop would not permit any kind of consultation about his successor.

Meanwhile the Apostolic Delegation has since 1972 followed closely the papal norms. One of the most recent cases has been that of the Archdiocese of Saint Louis which brought to conclusion in October 1979 a consultation that embraced the consultors, the pastoral commission, the council of priests, and the council of religious women. These four groups submitted reports through the retiring archbishop to the Apostolic Delegation which embodied their views concerning the current status of the archdiocese and its needs, along with a summary of the qualities they thought desirable in a new ordinary. These reports were intended to assist the Apostolic Delegation in choosing three names of potential successors to Cardinal John Carberry which Archbishop Jean Jadot would, in turn, submit to the Holy See, along with his personal recommendations.[7] Periodic consultations of a similar nature are carried out in other dioceses regarding auxiliary bishops, e.g., the Archdiocese of New York.

If the Saint Louis case represents the typical way in which the process of selection is conducted in the United States at present, there is always the possibility of exceptions to the rule. E.g., before his death in 1967 Cardinal Francis Spellman, Archbishop of New York, was able to name a large number of bishops by reason of his personal relationship to Pius XII. While it would be difficult to cite exact cases of this kind, it would be naïve to rule out the possibility of their ever happening again. The personal element will always remain an important factor in these matters. Moreover, there is the occasional instance where the resignation of an ordinary and the appointment of his successor are announced simultaneously, e.g., Seattle, Washington, in 1975, which suggests little consultation of a broad nature.

The papal norms—sustained by both the Apostolic Delegation and the National Conference of Catholic Bishops—do not allow for anything like a 'collective consultation'. Nor do they permit the initiation of the selecting process on the part of any group of priests, religious, or laity. Yet these norms do not necessarily constitute a final way of selecting bishops of the Latin Rite. They can, and in some particulars should, be changed. This pertains to the selecting of most auxiliary bishops which has been left largely to the ordinary. The weakness of such a selecting process is too evident to need elaboration, given the all too human tendency of ordinaries to choose auxiliaries who will reflect their own ideology, or even timid men whose qualities of leadership will not contrast unfavourably with those of the ordinary. Whether in the time ahead, therefore, groups like the Canon Law Society of America will succeed in convincing the NCCB that they should seek exceptions and changes for the American Church, remains to be seen. If the CLSA should fail in this regard there would seem to be no other responsible group of American Catholics who will succeed. In the meantime the process of selection of American bishops will in all likelihood continue to follow the pattern of that summarised above for the Archdiocese of Saint Louis.

The selection of bishops always has been—and will ever remain—of paramount importance for the Church. Few have emphasised the point more strongly than Saints Peter Canisius and Robert Bellarmine. One of the latter's early biographers summarised the matter in words that have pertinence in 1980 as much as they did for the time in which they were written. Of Bellarmine it was said:

'. . . his chief anxiety and the thing which he deemed of, perhaps, the greatest importance was the choice of bishops. He desired that extraordinary care should be exercised in their selection and demanded that this should be based solely on merit and holiness. . . .'[8]

*Notes*

1. 'The Brief *Ex hac apostolicae* of Pope Pius VI Erecting the Diocese of Baltimore and Appointing John Carroll as the First Bishop, 6 November 1789' John Tracy Ellis, ed., *Documents of American Catholic History* (Chicago 1967) I, 165.

2. The United States Government Declines to Commit Itself on a Bishop for Louisiana, 17-20 November 1806' *Ibid.* I, 187.

3. Anthony H. Deye 'Archbishop John Baptist Purcell of Cincinnati: Pre-Civil War Years' unpublished doctoral dissertation, University of Notre Dame (1959) pp. 60-61.

4. Gabriel Tissot, O.S.B. trans. and ed. *Ambroise de Milan. Traité sur L'Evangile de S. Luc.* (Paris 1956) p. 81. Leo I in a letter to Anastasius, Bishop of Thessalonica, after 4 January 446, stated: 'No one, of course, is to be consecrated against the wishes of the people and without their requesting it. Otherwise, the citizens will despise or hate the bishop they do not want and thus become less religious than they should, on the grounds that they were not permitted to have the man of their choice' Edmund Hunt, F.S.C. trans. *St Leo the Great. Letters* (New York 1957) p. 53.

5. William W. Bassett ed. *The Choosing of Bishops* (Hartford, Canon Law Society of America 1971).

6. 'The Selection of Bishops' *Priests' Forum* I (March-April 1979) 26. In spite of an open and direct invitation from Bishop Ernest J. Primeau, a majority of the priests of the diocese, 'did not submit names and, as a signature was not required, it was impossible to determine the validity of what was submitted' *op. cit.*

7. *Saint Louis Review* 26 October 1979 p. 1.

8. Daniello Bertoli, S.J., quoted by James Brodrick, S.J. *The Life and Works of Blessed Robert Francis Bellarmine, S.J., 1542-1621* (London 1928) I p. 453.

*Bibliography*

Bassett, William W., ed. *The Choosing of Bishops* (Hartford, Canon Law Society of America 1971). See here especially Robert Trisco 'The Variety of Procedures in Modern History' pp. 33-80.

Ellis, John Tracy 'On Selecting American Bishops' *Commonweal* 85 (10 March 1967) 643-649, and the same writer's essay, 'On Selecting Catholic Bishops for the United States' *The Critic* 26 (June-July 1969) 42-48

Provost, James H. 'Selection of Bishops—Does Anybody Care' *Chicago Studies* 18 (Summer 1979) 211-222.

Muriel Bowen

# The Appointment of Bishops in Britain since Vatican II

ONE OF the happier developments in the Church in Great Britain since Vatican II is the new interest in the appointment of bishops. Previously, with the exception here and there of priests in university staff rooms the feeling was always: 'The pope knows best'.

For some years before the controversial encyclical *Humanae Vitae*, the British had come to expect a changed attitude in Rome. Artificial birth control would be tolerated within marriage in certain circumstances. In 1964 Archbishop Thomas Roberts, S.J., former Archbishop of Bombay, who had a gift for bringing unwelcome issues into the open wrote in the progressive Catholic magazine *Search* that he could not understand the traditional teaching of the Church he loved. Next day he was almost everybody's friend! When *Humanae Vitae* did come lay Catholics and many priests did not blame the pope, but bishops who gave him bad advice. Serious mass circulation newspapers like *The Times, The Sunday Times*, and *The Observer* investigated week after week. Some bishops, notably Archbishop Cowdray of Southwark, defended the encyclical in pastorals expressed in the language of a century ago.

Cardinal Heenan, worried about the impression the Church was making in the newspapers, pleaded with other bishops for silence until the Bishops' Conference could make a statement. This document was, clearly, better. The informed individual conscience was pointed out, if not stressed. The hand of Bishop Christopher Butler, O.S.B., the only English bishop to make an impact on Vatican II, was to be seen in it.

However, public opinion was now unstoppable. Priests and laity began to send successive Papal Delegates an identikit of the sort of bishop they wanted. The newspapers printed letters on the issues of bishops and birth control. I counted 281 in *The Times, The Sunday Times, The Guardian*, and the Liverpool *Post* 1966-1969. The row on birth control which developed into questioning the appointment of bishops was without precedent in England.

After centuries of persecution caused by penal laws Catholic emancipation was granted by Parliament in 1829; the hierarchy was restored in 1850.

Cardinal Wiseman, Spanish born and Rome educated, became the first Archbishop of Westminster. He was a man of boundless enthusiasm for building up the Church and developing Roman devotions in preference to old English ones. He knew England not at all well.

Why did he get the job? He was Rector of the Venerable English College in Rome. He was the man the Vatican knew. The point is significant because a century later, in the

1950s, it was said and widely believed by priests in England that there were three qualifications for becoming an English bishop. To be properly ordained, of the male sex, and to have an association with the Venerable English College. Of the three it was said that only the first two could be dropped!

Several Archbishops of Westminster after Wiseman had been rectors of the college. Scores of bishops had been educated there. Many priests felt by the early 1970s that there was an urgent need of the bishops to be more representative of the Church and nation.

It was not that 'The Venerable' had the best candidates. But its proximity to the Vatican ensured that they were the best known.

At the time the hierarchy was restored a chapter with about ten canons in each diocese was established. When a bishopric became vacant, the chapter met with the metropolitan, or his deputy, to choose a *terna* of three names.

The names chosen were to be arranged not on the basis of the vote, but in alphabetical order and discussed by the bishops of the province. Then they were forwarded to Rome with comments on each candidate.

This, of course, was all in secret, so how much influence the chapter carried is not known. Nor is it known how much influence the canons had with a man like Cardinal Manning who followed Wiseman at Westminster (1865-1892). A brilliant administrator, he found it difficult to see the other person's point of view. According to E. S. Purcell, his biographer, he was apt to say of routine business 'the Chapter's opposition (to me) must displease God'. That opposition was hardly surprising as the Cardinal held the view that for bishops to drink wine at dinner or allow theatricals in convent girls' schools were 'hindrances to the spread of the Catholic Church in England'.

But in time the chapters got the strength of their preferences for different candidates known when a see became vacant. In April 1969 Archbishop Cardinale, Papal Delegate to Great Britain wrote me: 'Full details of the voting of the names proposed are sent to the Apostolic Delegation for transmission to the Sacred Congregation of Bishops'.

By 1968 the public were critical of bishops appointed as never before. The following year when auxiliary bishops were appointed to Liverpool and Northampton, they were criticised by priests and laity as 'too conservative . . . not sufficiently imbued with the spirit of Vatican II'.

Worried about the outcome of their diocese, the priests of Brentwood carried out a poll of all 171 priests in the diocese asking what sort of man they would like to replace their retired bishop. Brentwood is typical of England. It includes the London docks, one of the biggest car-making factories in Europe, rural villages, and seaside towns with many retired people from the professions and business.

*The Brentwood Report, 1969* consisted of the views of the 139 priests who responded. Theologically speaking 64 per cent wanted a 'reasonably progressive man'. The prospective bishop's attitude to ecumenism was important to 97 per cent. A more open attitude to women was thought desirable, and 84 per cent wanted 'certain women' (meaning religious) to be given a more active role by the bishop.

No less than 54 per cent thought the English system for selecting bishops bad or very bad: 'The cathedral chapter, not being an elected body, is not representative of the clergy, and the lay people have no say at all.''

The last point was no longer true. Archbishop Cardinale told me in 1969: 'The congregation is free to obtain information about the post to be filled and the candidates from any source . . . any person is free to approach the congregation with information, suggestions, etc.'

Nobody seems to have informed the public of that until I wrote it in *The Sunday Times*. A new bishop emerged from Rome as if on a tablet of stone.

The real problem lay further back. The essence of the problem was contained in a passage I wrote in *The Sunday Times*, September 1971: 'In the past 15 years individual bishops have been allowed a free hand in choosing their auxiliary bishops. All too often they have gone for quiet, industrious men of little distinction and less intelligent than themselves. That would have been all very well if Rome had not filled every vacant bishopric, with one exception, from the list of auxiliary bishops. As a result standards have fallen.'

Further interest in bishops' appointments was sparked off by the 1970 Anglican report *Church and State*. This stated that when an English see fell vacant, the Queen granted a licence to the dean and chapter, which was in the form of a letter 'containing the name of the person they should elect'. This was absurd. It has since been changed.

Cardinal Heenan, Archbishop of Westminster, worried at this point that control might get out of the hands of the bishops. In 1971 he introduced a procedure, so a list of *episcopabiles* was kept by the National Bishops' Conference and reviewed annually.

It was obvious to me that the system of selection was inadequate in two respects. Neither laity nor priests had more than inadequate knowledge to advise. They were unaware what candidates could contribute nationally, or at diocesan level. The bishops on the congregation had to rely virtually entirely on Vatican information on men from outside their own country.

Three friends of mine served on the Congregation of Bishops through most of the 1970s, Cardinals Heenan, Conway and Wright and I had several long talks with them on how the system worked. Cardinal Heenan told of Vatican messengers bringing him dossiers on candidates to the English College the night before the Congregation met. It left no time for further independent enquiry.

What contribution could he make, I asked, when a bishop was being appointed in, say Upper Volta? 'I keep silence, read my papers, write my letters.' When an English bishop is being appointed? 'I make clear whom we consider the best man.' Cardinal Conway said he too always attended when there were Irish appointments, but when Westminster became vacant Archbishop Dwyer (then on the Congregation) told me he would not be attending. It 'wasn't protocol', he informed me when appointments were being made in one's own country.

Cardinal John Wright who served on the Congregation for almost a decade saw it change significantly. Before his death in 1979 he told me: 'Now it's reached the point where everybody falls over backwards to meet the wishes of the local church. People like myself with wider experience are ignored.'

In 1973 Archbishop Bruno Heim was appointed Papal Delegate in Britain. He is Swiss, speaks good English, is a good listener, an expert gardener (the English hobby is gardening), and a man of unbounded energy. He let it be known that he wanted every Catholic in the pew to feel free to write to him and make their views known before a bishop is appointed. Everybody knows the machinery is not the greatest but he has a real will to make it work.

When Westminster became vacant he got over 800 letters.

The first mention of Cardinal Hume who was appointed, and who is now President of the European bishops, was in an article of mine in *The Sunday Times*, September 1975. I had never heard of Abbot Hume of the Benedictines when I wrote the article. The paper decided to run a poll picking 120 names at random from the *Catholic Directory* and spoke to 89. He turned out to be the second most favoured person. I was struck by the emphasis placed on his spirituality. He was also favoured by people who regarded him as having great gifts in reconciling differences over liturgy and theology within the Benedictine Order.

Archbishop Heim told the editor of *The Ampleforth Jounal*: 'In writing about the appointment you must start with Muriel Bowen—she first brought his name to public notice.'

I only mention this to show that the laity *can* be influential even when they do not set out with that intention. My aim was to find six people who were well supported and give all relevant facts.

Now the need in Britain is to get a few English bishops appointed who have a gift for communication so that the Church can make an impact direct in the TV and the mass media. Since the death of Cardinal Heenan we lack a man who is such that when he speaks, the country takes notice.

Richard Auwerda

# Becoming a Bishop in the Netherlands since Vatican II

WITHIN sixteen months after the final session of 8 December 1965 of the Second Vatican Council, three of the seven Dutch bishops who had taken part in the Council were dead. Wilhelmus Bekkers of Den Bosch, who was fifty-six years old when he died, had already been ill for some time. Johannes van Dodewaard of Haarlem, who was fifty-two, and Cornelis de Vet of Breda, who was forty-nine, both died suddenly.

The way in which a new bishop is appointed to a Dutch diocese is not simply determined by the general directives that are valid for the whole Church. From the time of the Reformation until the middle of the nineteenth century, the Netherlands had no bishops of its own and was regarded by Rome as a missionary country. Its hierarchy was restored in 1853,[1] but it continued to come under the authority of the Roman *Propaganda* until as late as 1908 and to be treated as a missionary country that could not stand on its own feet.

The Dutch province of the Church has retained one 'privilege' attached to this status. That is that three candidates may be nominated by the cathedral chapter of the diocese in which the bishop's see is vacant and their names sent to Rome.[2] This does not mean that the nominating authority also has to choose one of the men whose name has been suggested. The canons make a list with the names of their candidates in order of preference. This proposal is then sent in duplicate to the college of bishops. One copy is sent on without change. The other has notes and comments written on it and possibly the readers' own candidates added to it.

Both the proposal sent by the chapter and that from the college of bishops are taken to the Vatican by the papal representative in the Netherlands.[3] He is the third advisory authority and in fact his advice carries the greatest weight, although this may only be because he is situated a floor higher as the advisory lift goes up from the Netherlands to the Vatican City. He is able, first, to move one or more candidates into a better position and, secondly, to comment on all those whose names have been put forward by the chapter and the college of bishops. He does not need to justify his advice or even to inform one of the other advisory authorities, with the result that he in fact does neither.

What is more, there is an unwritten tradition in the Netherlands that a bishop always comes from the clergy of his own diocese. The name of a regular priest has occasionally appeared on a nomination, but since 1853 the old rule has never been broken. The idea of the 'career bishop' who is able to come from a small or poor diocese to a more 'important' see is also unknown in the Netherlands.

On the basis of these written and unwritten rules, a new bishop was found for all three vacant sees within about six months in 1966 and 1967, but events followed a course that was slightly different from that followed in the past. Because of the recent Council, a new vision of the bishop's office was becoming widely accepted and there were cautious signs of this when the diocese of Haarlem, which was the first of three to lose its bishop at this time, had to prepare for the appointment of a new bishop.

The sudden and quite unexpected death of Bishop van Dodewaard on 9 March 1966 meant that there was not much time to evolve a procedure that would make it possible for more than simply the members of the cathedral chapter to work together on the nomination. There was no real precedent for the situation. The canons therefore had to improvise and they decided that each one of them should sound out the opinions of as many priests as possible within the circle of his own acquaintances.

One of them, Dean J. Kraakman of Alkmaar, told a local newspaper what was proposed and at once the vicar and provost of the chapter, Martin Groot, who had been vicar general under the late bishop, received a warning from the papal nuncio that consultation among a wide circle had never been the practice and that a nomination based on such a procedure would not make a good impression. The members of the chapter were startled, but they went ahead with the consultation, although very cautiously indeed.

It is sometimes difficult to ascertain afterwards whether a bishop who was nominated by the cathedral chapter and the other bishops was in fact appointed and, if so, whether that bishop was their first choice or Rome's. All those concerned are always bound to secrecy and generally speaking they kept to this. All the same, there is every reason to assume that the present vicar general of the diocese, Harry Kuipers, was the chapter's first choice at that time and that the new bishop, Theo Zwartkruis, who was Dean of Haarlem at the time, was second on the list. Kuipers seems to have been passed over because of the way in which he dealt, as Official, with divorced Catholics who wanted to remarry, thus putting into practice a concept of ecclesiastical law that was at that time not acceptable to the Vatican.

Bishop Bekkers was sick for a month before he died on 9 May 1966. The diocese was therefore better prepared for the question of how to involve the community in the choice of a successor. The need to do this was even then much greater in the Diocese of Den Bosch than elsewhere because Bekkers, who was known in the Netherlands as the 'Dutch John XXIII', had been a living model of a bishop of the kind that many people had come to know during the Council—the high-ranking office-bearer who was much more of a guide, exponent and binding factor of the Church community in the way of an authority placed above that community.

There were nine canons of the chapter at that time and they invited everyone, including non-Catholics, to co-operate so that a justified nomination could be sent to Rome. Through the nuncio in The Hague, the Vatican asked again and again for information. It became clear that Rome was afraid that the pope's freedom of choice would be subjected to pressure.

The chapter asked for an answer to two questions in particular. The first was: What are your expectations of the new bishop? The second was: Whom do you regard as possible candidates? The operation was certainly not seen as a survey or a ballot. It was an attempt to sound opinions in an informal way, an invitation to cooperate spontaneously.

It was estimated that at least ten thousand people, many of them working in groups, put forward suggestions. Many of them were not Catholics. What emerged as the most important qualities that the new bishop should have was that he would be cooperative and would bind all those who thought differently together, that he would act as a catalyst and an interpreter in the life of the Church community and that everyone would therefore recognise himself or herself in him and feel secure with him. It is no longer a secret that most of the suggestions indicated Johannes Bluyssen, who had been Bekkers' coadjutor since 1961. Rome respected the people's wish and Bluyssen became Bishop of Den Bosch.

When he was installed, he declared: 'I believe that I have been personally commissioned by Christ, but I also believe that this commission has in the first place come to me from and through the Church. That is why a bishop will be able to rely on his authority the more firmly he is rooted among his people.'[4]

The following year, Bishop de Vet of Breda died suddenly and the chapter of that diocese also wanted to sound out opinions and incorporate the findings into the nomination for a successor. The advice was therefore sought of the members of the diocesan pastoral council, which at that time consisted, in normal circumstances, of the bishop and the nine members of his chapter, forty-five priests, sixteen religious and thirty lay people. At the same time, the chapter also make it known that Bishop de Vet's successor would be a man who would be able to continue the work of renewal that his predecessor had begun.[5] This intention met with such general agreement that only thirty-four members of the pastoral council responded to the chapter's invitation.[6] By common consent, Hubertus Ernst, the provost of the chapter and its vicar, was thought to be the most suitable candidate. It was widely expected that his name would be placed at the top of the list of nominations and in fact both the chapter and Rome did exactly this.

In October 1968, Petrus Nierman resigned as Bishop of Groningen for reasons of health. In this diocese too, the chapter 'appealed to everyone who felt involved in the life of the Church' to make known what expectations they had of a bishop 'at this time and in this diocese'.[7] The chapter turned especially in this instance to the pastoral council and the council of priests, asking the members of each to provide a profile of the kind of man they were looking for. There were numerous responses and many included names of suggested candidates.

The chapter placed the names of three priests who were members of the diocese on the list, but the man who was appointed was Johannes Möller, who was a priest in the archdiocese of Utrecht and was at the time teaching philosophy to priests in training at Utrecht. This choice was formally a departure from the tradition in the Netherlands, according to which a priest from the diocese is always made bishop of that diocese. The justification of this unwritten tradition has always been that it guarantees that the bishop will know the clergy of the diocese. This guarantee was present in the case of Möller, however, because the diocese of Groningen and the archdioces of Utrecht had formed a single diocese until only ten years before. The priests of both dioceses therefore knew each other and most of them had been trained at the place where Möller was teaching.

This does not, however, explain why Rome chose to ignore the nominations made by the chapter. A fairly widely accepted explanation is that Cardinal Alfrink wanted to give his ex-student Möller the chance to have episcopal experience so that he would be in the running if it came to a decision about a successor to the archbishop's see.

It was no trouble for Alfrink to get Möller into the college of bishops. It is a good indication of the great authority that he enjoyed in the Vatican at the time that he was able to win Rome over to his side on behalf of his favourite candidate. If historians later criticise the papal representative in The Hague in the case of the appointments in Rotterdam and Roermond and say that he ignored the recommendations of the chapters in each of these dioceses, they will also have to remember that Angelo Felici was not the first man to have behaved in this way.

The appointments of the new Bishops of Rotterdam and Roermond are the most sensational in the history of the Dutch Church for more than a century. When Martinus

Jansen retired as Bishop of Rotterdam for health reasons, the most extensive consultation that has ever taken place in connection with the choice of a bishop in the
Netherlands was set afoot. There were tens of thousands of responses to the request to
help in outlining the profile of a bishop who was really wanted. The preference was for a
man who was first and foremost a shepherd of his flock who was orientated towards the
future and able to cooperate with and listen to others. A chain of enquiry took place
which passed through the hands of the pastoral council, the priests of the diocese and
many others who were directly involved in the life of the Church and ended with the
chapter. The result was that a regular priest who was vicar-general in the diocese,
Cornelis Braun, was the first name on the list of nominations. The new bishop, who was
appointed on 30 December 1970, was, however, Dr A. Simonis. His name had not
appeared among the three suggested by the diocese, although he had been a candidate
proposed by a number of conservatives. He did not fit into the profile, so his name had
been dropped.

A storm of protests followed, the fire being fanned by a number of statements made
by the new bishop which showed clearly that he strongly supported, for example,
priestly celibacy and a strict observation of the teaching of *Humanae Vitae*. The deans
asked him not to accept his appointment. The members of the central committee of the
diocesan pastoral council all resigned. There was a statement from the nunciature that
the list of candidates had been fraudulently prepared. Finally, the Dutch bishops had
very detailed conversations with their new colleague before deciding to consecrate him.

Optimists thought that the appointment of Bishop Simonis to Rotterdam was an
industrial accident. Like Bishop Simonis' predecessor in Rotterdam, the Bishop of
Roermond, P. Moors, asked to be allowed to resign because of his health. Nothing
daunted, the diocese of Roermond began the task of preparing for a new bishop. The
news that Bishop Moors' resignation had been accepted by the Vatican was published
on the day after Bishop Simonis' nomination had been made public.

Roermond's original plan for consultation was very similar to Rotterdam's, but,
because of the example of Rotterdam, where the procedure had produced quite the
wrong result, Roermond decided to regard the candidates whose names emerged from
the consultation not as nominations that had to be accepted by the chapter, but merely
as suggestions. The nunciature, however, did not want the chapter to be given any names
at all by the pastoral council or other bodies. Roermond therefore confined itself to
providing no more than a profile of the type of bishop the diocese wanted and left the
rest to the chapter, in the firm expectation that the suggestions would be taken seriously.

The chapter produced a list, based on these suggestions, containing the names of
three moderately progressive candidates, because these fitted in best with the expectations of the people. Two names were held in reserve, in case Rome found the others
unacceptable and wanted to compromise with an 'interim pope'. There was, then, a clear
assumption that the Vatican would take part in consultations if it found Roermond's
nomination unacceptable. This did not happen. The diocese's nomination was ignored
and there was no consultation. Dr Johannes Gijsen was named Bishop of Roermond on
22 January 1972.

This was the beginning of a period characterised by polarisation, non-
communication, rejection, disintegration, authoritarian decisions and condemnations,
first within the diocese of Roermond itself and later at a national level. The bishop
withdrew from many national Christian organisations and avoided even normal col-
laboration with his fellow-bishops.

In the meantime, Cardinal Alfrink sought resignation in 1975, when he had reached
the age of seventy-five. For the fourth time in succession, the nomination was sent to
Rome, this time by the chapter of the archdiocese of Utrecht, which was not honoured.
The man appointed was Cardinal Willebrands, originally from the diocese of Haarlem.

He became the head of the Dutch Church while retaining his function as leader of the Vatican department for ecumenism, a post which committed him to numerous journeys all over the world. The pastoral council of the archdiocese was right to complain—its members had looked forward not only to a Bishop of Utrecht, but also to a leader of the Dutch Church.

There was considerable tension in the Conference of Bishops when it was headed by Alfrink, but when he was succeeded by Willebrands this tension increased. Now there are very few unanimous decisions made by the bishops. There are also quite frequent cases of failure in collective leadership, some of which are made public, as, for example, when the bishops were recently discussing how to find a way of working together and Bishop Gijsen, without consulting his colleagues, told a weekly newspaper that it was time for the pope to intervene in the Church in the Netherlands[8]. In the same interview, he said—while the Bishops' Conference was discussing the whole problem of abortion—that he would refuse to admit Catholic politicians to the sacraments if they collaborated in any measures to legalise abortion.

All this has proved too much for most of the other Dutch bishops. Willebrands consulted with Pope John Paul II who did not do what Gijsen had wanted, that is, intervene, but asked the bishops themselves to suggest a way out of the problem. Willebrands' idea was to hold a special Dutch synod.

The real question is, why were bishops with such clearly conservative attitudes appointed to Rotterdam and Roermond? The pastoral leadership of the united and unanimous college of Dutch bishops that was evident for so long after the Second Vatican Council was always a thorn in Rome's flesh. Many factors contributed to the increasingly bad relationship—the New ('Dutch') Catechism of 1966, the pastoral reaction of the Dutch bishops to *Humanae Vitae* in 1968 and finally the Dutch Pastoral Council, the policy-making organisation of the Church in the Netherlands, consisting of bishops, priests, religious and lay people, which was intended to draw the practical conclusions from the Second Vatican Council. The Pastoral Council's public demand that the question of obligatory celibacy for priests should be discussed at world level gave rise to very bad feeling in the Vatican. Indeed, the whole idea of national consultation and of encroaching on the bishops' leadership, even in free discussion, through the medium of various institutions, was very displeasing to Rome, where it was feared that the individual appeal to the bishops' personal sense of responsibility would be diminished in this way.

The appointment of notorious conservatives (Simonis prefers to describe himself as a 'strict' Catholic, thus borrowing a word from the Calvinist vocabulary) was clearly an attempt to correct the bishops' leadership. Two such bishops were added to the Dutch college in order to give a specific group in the Dutch Church its own voice in the hierarchy.

The result, however, was that polarisation was introduced into the college of bishops. Alfrink expressed his criticism of the situation when Simonis was consecrated in the following way: 'After many years' experience, I think I can say that, in the present situation, the main burden and care of a bishop's office is that he has to build bridges on all sides. It would be easy if he could identify himself with one particular group among his flock, but he is the shepherd of the whole flock.'[9] He also had this to say, on the same occasion, about the consternation caused by the appointment of Simonis: 'It has done a great deal of harm to the Church and has undermined confidence in the Church's authority. The most regrettable aspect of the affair is that it could have been avoided if different paths had been followed. A repetition of this situation must at all costs be avoided.'

But barely a year later the situation was in fact repeated in Roermond and there are quite a few Catholics in the Netherlands who regard the appointment to the see of

Utrecht in 1975 as a further repetition. The main theme of the 1980 synod of Dutch bishops was how to improve the *communio* of the Church. More violence was done to that *communio* by the appointments of Simonis and Gijsen than by any other events in recent years. It was logical enough that an attempt should have been made during the synod to include among the conclusions that the nominations made in the future by the competent Dutch authorities to vacant episcopal sees should be taken seriously by Rome. This attempt failed.

In an opinion survey held in the Netherlands before the Roman synod in January 1980, it emerged that only 24 per cent of Dutch Roman Catholics recognised themselves in the leadership of Bishop Bluyssen of Den Bosch and that all the other Dutch bishops scored less than 10 per cent. Of all the Catholics in the Netherlands, as many as 53 per cent were not in sympathy with any of the bishops.[10]

*Translated by David Smith*

*Notes*

1. Pope Pius IX's breve *Ex qua die* of 1853 set up five dioceses in the Netherlands: Utrecht (the archdiocese), Haarlem, Breda, Den Bosch and Roermond. In 1956, two dioceses (Haarlem and Utrecht) were each divided into two, giving two new dioceses, Rotterdam and Groningen respectively.

2. Instruction of the Congregatio de Propaganda Fide, 17 July 1858.

3. His task, as defined in the 'Norms concerning those who are to be promoted to the office of bishop in the Latin Church', published on 25 March 1972 by the Council for Public Affairs in the Church, had been practised for years in the Netherlands. According to Article 29, 'Before a candidate is declared to have been chosen as a bishop, the Apostolic See must have instituted a careful and detailed investigation into him. . . . The task of carrying out this investigation is entrusted to the papal envoy, who is to inquire among the clergy—bishops, priests and religious. Well informed and really outstanding lay people, who, from their own knowledge, have useful information to impart concerning the candidate, may also be examined'.

4. *De Volkskrant* (25 April 1966).

5. *Ibid.* (21 November 1966).

6. Report on the statements made by the members of the diocesan pastoral council, 8 May 1967 (*Opbouw* [17 December 1967]).

7. Letter from the cathedral chapter of Breda to the diocesan pastoral council, 17 November 1968 (see *Opbouw* [17 December 1967]).

8. *Elseviers Magazine* (20 January 1979).

9. *Archief van de Kerken* 26 (2 April 1971) col. 303-304.

10. NIPO survey, undertaken by Dutch Television and published on 11 December 1979.

# Hans Küng

# The Freedom of the Election of the Bishop in Basel

## 1. AS IT NOW IS

THE SWISS diocese of Basel differs from most other dioceses in the world in that the bishop is elected by the diocesan clergy of the cathedral chapter alone, without any interference from official agencies in Rome. It is only afterwards that Rome confirms the vote. The governing bodies of the local cantons therefore enjoy a limited power of veto, but this has not been excercised for a long time.

The legal basis for this election of the bishop in the diocese of Basel is the series of treaties between the governing bodies of the relevant cantons and the Holy See.[1] There is no doubt about the legal position of the cathedral chapter and the diocesan canons. The State treaty in question provides as follows: 'The canons of the cathedral who constitute the episcopal senate have the right to elect the bishop from among the clergy of the diocese. The person elected bishop will be confirmed in office by the Holy Father as soon as the canonical formalities have been completed according to the forms of the Church customary in Switzerland' (compare art. 5). The Apostolic Bull of Leo XII of 7 May 1828 confirms this and adds that when the papal confirmation cannot for any reason follow, it is again not the pope but the cathedral chapter which must proceed to a new election.

It follows that the right of election belongs unequivocally to the cathedral senate of the diocese, which carries out the election without consulting or informing Rome in any way. And the phrase 'according to the forms of the Church customary in Switzerland' refers to that cooperation with the cantons of the diocese which was explicitly recognised in papal briefs: 'The Church flourishes when government and priesthood agree together.' What this means, according to the same brief of Leo XII dated 15 September 1828, is that no candidates should be elected who are *gubernio minus grati*, i.e., who are not acceptable to the cantonal governments.[2]

These ancient rights of the cathedral chapter and the cantons of the diocese alike which have been acknowledged by Rome in this way and which do not envisage Rome being involved in the information process to the slightest degree have, naturally, been respected in every episcopal election to date. They are comprehensively laid down in the *Statuta Capituli Ecclesiae Cathedralis Basilensis* which have been explicitly confirmed with only minor modifications in the recent codification of Church law. These statutes[3] specify the method of election in a manner that acknowledges the traditional rights both of the diocesan cantons and of the cathedral chapter in a most emphatic way.

The election of the bishop must take place within three months.[4] The vicar of the cathedral chapter negotiates the determination of the date of the election with the governing bodies of the cantons.[5] Consultation with the governing bodies must be completed before the solemn vote.[6] In this way the chapter has to give precedence to the candidates who are not 'minus grati'[7] Rome plays no part in this consultation. Where the election has to be repeated or where the pope does not approve, the chapter becomes competent again.[8] The procedure of the election has to be strictly observed down to the last detail. When the election has been completed, the provost of the cathedral or his deputy declares: 'In my own name and in that of the cathedral senate of Basel I announce and proclaim that the Right Reverend N. N. has been elected to be bishop and pastor of the Church in Basel in the name of the Father, and of the Son and of the Holy Spirit. Amen.'[10] By way of conclusion the election has to be promulgated in the cathedral so that the Te Deum can be solemnly sung and the election be closed with this festive song of thanks.[11] Should the person elected not be there, he should be informed of the election straightaway and asked whether he accepts.[12] He must signify this within eight days or else refuse.[13] The official authentication of the election, duly signed by all the elective members of the cathedral chapter, together with the necessary attestation of the qualification of the person elected, must then be sent to the pope in the usual way.[14] Once the Holy See has signified its approval, the solemn consecration of the bishop can follow.[15]

It is a matter for regret that on the occasion of the election of the last bishop (in 1967) the chapter yielded to the massive pressure from the Roman curia and the nunciature. Instead of announcing the result of the election in the way the concordat and custom required, the chapter bound itself under oath to silence, at first kept the name of the person elected secret, informed the curia instead of the clergy and the people and secured its nihil obstat before it informed the person elected publicly. It was as if it were asking too much to expect the Holy See to ratify a perfectly legal election (and not a fait accompli). The incidental irony of the thing was that because of Rome's indiscretions the clergy and people had to get the name of the person elected, not from the cathedral chapter, as envisaged by the concordat, but from the press. We can only hope that for the next election there will be a strict adherence to the letter and the spirit of the concordat and to traditional procedure and that there is no yielding to pressure. For, apart from the anachronistic (but nowadays undangerous) possibility of interference by the State, the Basel regime stands out for having behind it not only Vatican II but the old Catholic tradition: The election of the bishop through a representative organ of the diocese.

We should note that both in its actual law and in its spirit this procedure anticipated much of what Vatican II set great store by (without, of course, drawing out the practical consequences for the election of bishops): (a) the theological and practical importance of the local and particular churches, the diocese and the community;[16] (b) the furtherance of decentralisation, which requires a divesting of power over the churches in individual countries on the part of the Roman curia;[17] (c) the furtherance of the reform of the curia, which is a matter not of widening the competence of the curia over the dioceses of individual countries but, on the contrary, of the inclusion of representatives of the different countries in the central administration of the Church;[18] (d) the stricter delimitation or limitation of the powers of the nuncios as desired by the Council: 'The Fathers also eagerly desire that, in view of the pastoral role proper to bishops, the office of legates of the Roman Pontiff be more precisely determined.'[19]

## 2. AS IT WAS

In order to understand these conclusions of Vatican II in historical perspective we should recall that they represent a bridgehead against Roman centralism, directiveness and absolutism as these have held sway in the West since the Gregorian reform and the high Middle Ages, and reached its highest point in the period after Vatican I with the new codification of canon law. At the same time these resolutions represent not daring 'innovations' but a return to tradition, the good, old tradition. The election of bishops is precisely an outstanding example of how things used to be. From the very beginning the election of a bishop expressed the awareness that the Church is not a clerical hierarchy of office but the whole community of believers, the whole people of God. In primitive Christianity the bishop was elected by clergy and people. The greatest bishops in all times like Ambrose of Milan and Augustine of Hippo were decisively elected by the people. *'Nos eligimus eum'*—'We elect him'—ran the formula of the people's accla-mation in the Latin countries. Nor was it the Bishop of Rome but neighbouring bishops who cooperated to give their sanction. The right to confirm and consecrate was gien later according to the definitions of the first ecumenical Council of Nicaea not to the See of Rome but to the metropolitan of the relevant Church province. We cannot here go into the way in which local princes later came to have a share in filling the bishop's see and the way in which the biblically grounded right of the ecclesial people came to be more and more restricted. The reform movement of the Middle Ages nevertheless demanded the free election of bishops and clergy and people (this was what Leo IX demanded at the Synod of Rome in 1049). The freedom of election of bishops was thoroughly secured at least in relation to the princes in the investiture struggle. At the same time, the ever-increasing power of the cathedral chapter meant that the lower clergy and the laity were correspondingly excluded. Whereas in the beginning the cathedral chapter had only to agree to an election, it came more and more to determine it. The cathedral chapter's right of election was quite general by the end of the twelfth century and was laid down for the whole Church by the mightiest pope of the Middle Ages, Innocent III.

During the first few centuries the influence of the Bishop of Rome on the election of bishops did not extend substantially further than the rights he enjoyed as metropolitan and patriarch and it was only in the ninth century that he became involved regularly where there were complications (removal, replacement, conflicts about the election). But though the development favoured by the papacy which we have sketched above, the right of confirmation and ordination fell more and more into the hands of the Roman see. From the high Middle Ages onwards the right of ratification was often used in order to exert pressure on the electoral process. The end result was the system of reservations, according to which the popes kept the filling of the bishops' sees to themselves: first of all in isolated cases, then in certain defined sees and finally, from the fourteenth century onwards (under the Avignon Pope Urban V, 1363) quite generally.

In this way the electoral right of the cathedral chapter was whittled away and in due course abolished by law. It was only after the Western schism and in the conflict about the Council of Basel that the cathedral chapter was again recognised through the Concordat of Vienna in 1448 to have at least a limited right to elect the bishop. This did not stop the development of a manifold right of nomination on the part of the king or lord (or at least a right of qualification: *personae minus gratae*). With the downfall of the Catholic ruling houses these rights largely disappeared. The way was thereby made quite free for that general papal nomination of bishops which had long been prepared and which was not officially enshrined in the new Code of Canon Law (unilaterally proclaimed by Rome in 1918 without any say or even consultation on the part of the bishops and the Church).

The at present unlimited right of the Swiss dioceses of Basel, Chur and St Gallen (as well as Olmütz) to elect their own bishops remained the great exception. It is only in the Eastern churches linked with Rome that the right to fill the see derived from the early Church has remained partially operative and has recently been written into the new Code of Canon Law for the Eastern churches: As a general rule, the bishop is elected by the synod of bishops of the patriarchate. At the same time the freedom of vote is diluted (an instructive example!) in so far as the list of candidates has to be approved by Rome beforehand!

### 3. AS IT OUGHT TO BE

History makes it quite clear that the great freedom of the right to elect the bishop in Basel is, practically speaking, in the entire Catholic Church today a unique example not only of the greater freedom that prevailed in earlier times but of that which ought to obtain in the line of Vatican II in all dioceses of the Catholic Church.

It goes without saying that this particular way of conducting an election—particularly in regard to the anachronistic cooperation of the organs of state—is not ideal. Nevertheless the electoral procedure of the diocese of Basel is the nearest thing there is to the original and normative conception of the Church as well as to the new order envisaged by Vatican II. It represents an important and seminal growth-point for a possible new regime of episcopal election in the spirit of Vatican II: a reintegration of clergy and laity on the model of the old Church. This is not the place to expound how this is to happen in detail. What we can envisage immediately is an election in the future which involves not only the cathedral chapter but elected representatives of the clergy and laity of the various deaneries. We can also envisage an election operating through a diocesan council composed of clergy and layfolk in accordance with the directives of Vatican II.

*Translated by John Maxwell*

*Notes*

1. The treaties of 26 March 1828, contracted between the cantonal governments of Luzern, Bern, Solothurn and Zug and the Holy See, represented by the apostolic Internuncio Gizzi (to which should be added the treaty with Aargau in 1828, with Thurgau in 1929, and later with Basel).

2. See also the brief of 16 December 1831.

3. See heading II, B on the election of the bishop.

4. Art. 74.

5. Art. 75; 76.

6. Art. 78.

7. This can be established in various ways: See Art. 79 and the references therein cited to the relevant papal briefs.

8. Art. 81, with its reference to the relevant brief of 7th May 1828.

9. Arts. 82-89.

10. Art. 90.

11. Art. 91.

12. Art. 92.

13. Art. 93.

14. Art. 94.

15. Art. 95.

16. See in particular the Constitution on the Church, *Lumen Gentium*, § 26, and the Decree on the Bishops' Pastoral Office in the Church, *Christus Dominus,* e.g. § 27.

17. The setting up of Episcopal Conferences, etc; see *Christus Dominus,* §§ 36-38.

18. See *Christus Dominus* §§ 9-10.

19. *Christus Dominus* § 9; see also § 10.

# Contributors

RICHARD AUWERDA is a journalist who writes for *De Volkskrant*, a national newspaper which is published daily in Amsterdam. Since the Second Vatican Council, he has specialised in Church matters. Among his works are *Dossier Schillebeeckx* (1969) and *Johannes Gijsen, omstreden bisschop* (1973).

JEAN BERNHARD was born in 1914 at Ribeauvillé, Upper Rhine. He is professor of canon law at the University of Human Sciences in Strasbourg and has been director of the Institut de Droit Canonique since 1970. He is also Officialis in the diocese of Strasbourg. In 1951 he founded and still edits the *Revue de Droit Canonique*. He has taken part in the work of the pontifical commission for the revision of canon law. He has published *La Forme primitive de la collection en deux livres, source de la collection en 74 titres et de la collection d'Anselme de Lucques*.

MURIEL BOWEN has written on Catholic affairs in *The Sunday Times*, London, since 1966. This is a serious mass-circulation newspaper. In 1979 she was engaged on a *Sunday Times* book on the first year of Pope John Paul and travelled on his trips round Italy, and in Ireland and the United States.

GIOVANNI CERETI was born in Genoa in 1933. He first gained a degree in civil law from Genoa University and followed this up with theological studies at Genoa Seminary (and afterwards at the Gregorian University). He was ordained priest in 1960 and since then he has divided his life between pastoral ministry and reflection on the faith and life in the Church. His works include *Vivere la Chiesa* (1962); *Commento al decreto sull'ecumenismo* (1966); *Matrimonio ed indissolubilita: nuove prospettive* (1971); *Divorzia nuove nozze e penitenza nella chiesa primitiva* (1977).

LAMBERTO DE ECHEVERRÍA was born in 1918 in Vitoria, Spain, and ordained in 1941. He studied civil and canon law at Salamanca, and has lectured at both the State and the Pontifical universities there. His pastoral experience has been long and varied: founder and director of the clerical review *Uncunable*; director of the Pastoral Institute at Salamanca; a frequent contributor to the *Revista española de Derecho conónico*. His last published work was a study of the 750 years of the 'university oratory' of Salamanca, and he is now preparing the fourth edition of his *Ascetica del hombre de la calle* (Asceticism for the Man in the Street).

JOHN TRACY ELLIS is professorial lecturer in Church history in The Catholic University of America; his specialisation has been the history of American Catholicism.

JEAN GAUDEMET was born in Dijon, France, in 1908. He has been professor of Roman law at the universities of Grenoble, Strasburg and Paris as well as at the Institut de Droit Canonique of Strasburg. He is consultor to the papal commissions for the revision of the Code of Canon Law and of the code of Eastern law. His principal works on Church law and institutions include *L'Empire chrétien et ses destinées en Occident du XIe au XIIIe siecle* (1944), *La Formation du droit séculier et du droit de l'Eglise aux IVe et Ve siècles* (1979), *Conciles Gaulois du IVe siecle* (1977).

PATRICK GRANFIELD was born in 1930. He studied at the Pontifical Institute of St Anselm in Rome and at The Catholic University of America in Washington. Doctor of philosophy and doctor of theology, he teaches systematic theology at The Catholic University of America. Among his published works are: *Theologians at Work* (1967), *Ecclesial Cybernetics: A Study of Democracy in the Church* (1973), and *The Papacy in Transition* (1980).

JEAN-LOUIS HAROUEL was born in 1944, studied law in Paris at the Institut d'Etudes Politiques and the Ecole Pratique des Hautes Etudes, passed the *Agrégation* in law in 1977 and now teaches at the University of Poitiers. His writings include historical studies of town planning and work on the selection of bishops according to contemporary law.

EDWARD J. KILMARTIN, S.J., is professor of theology and director of the graduate programme in liturgical studies at the University of Notre Dame. His published works include studies on the history and theology of the Lord's Supper and Ordained Ministry.

HANS KÜNG was born in Sursee, Luzern, Switzerland, in 1928. He qualified in philosophy and theology at the Gregorian University, Rome, and gained his doctorate at the Institut Catholique, Paris. After two years pastoral work in Luzern, he started teaching first in the University of Münster then in Tübingen, where he has been professor of dogmatics and ecumenical theology since 1963 as well as director of the institute for ecumenical research. He has lectured widely in universities in Europe, America, Asia and Australia. He is a member of the editorial board of *Concilium*, editor of *Theologische Quartalschrift* and author of numerous books such as *Justification* (1964), *Structures of the Church* (1965), *Infallible? An Inquiry* (1971), *On Being a Christian* (1977).

JOSEPH LÉCUYER was born on 14 August 1912 at Kerfourn in France. He entered the Congregation of the Holy Spirit in 1930 and graduated in philosophy and theology at the Gregorian University in Rome. For many years now, he has been the director of the French Seminary in Rome and has been teaching at the Theological Faculty of the Gregorian and of St Anselm. He has written articles for various specialist journals, dictionaries and symposia. His main works include *Le Sacerdoce dans le mystère du Christ* (Paris 1957); *Le Sacrifice de la Nouvelle Alliance* (Le Puy and Lyons 1964) and *Etudes sur la collégialité épiscopale* (Le Puy and Lyons 1964).

JEAN RÉMY was born in Soumange, Belgium, in 1928 and studied at the University of Louvain, from which he holds a first degree in philosophy and a doctorate in economics. He is professor in the faculty of political and social science in the University of Louvain and director of the university's Centre for Urban and Rural Sociology. He has written widely on Christianity in an urban setting.

BERNHARD SCHIMMELPFENNIG was born on 14 June 1938 in Berlin, where he studied history, German language and literature and American prehistory. Following study and research in Italy, France and Spain he has since 1971 been professor of medieval history at the Free University of Berlin. In the field of Church history he has among other things published various studies on papal ceremonial and on papal history in the later middle ages, as well as studies on the situation of priests' sons and on the Spanish Holy Years.

PETER STOCKMEIER was born in Hemhof, near Rosenheim, in Upper Bavaria in 1925. After wartime military service, studies in theology and history at Münich and a spell as a university chaplain from 1952 until 1956, in 1958 he became a lecturer, and in 1962 a professor, at the Pädagogische Hochschule Pasing of the University of Münich. From 1964 until 1966 he was professor of Church History in the Theological Faculty of the University of Trier, and from 1966 until 1969 he was professor of Ancient Church History, Patrology and Christian Archaeology at the University of Tübingen. Since 1 October 1969 he has been ordinarius professor in the Institute for Church History at the University of Munich with the chair of ancient church history, patrology and Christian archaeology.

HARTMUT ZAPP was born in Säckingen in 1939. Postgraduate studies included work at the Institute of Medieval Canon Law and at Yale. He is now Privatdozent in the field of canon law and the history of canon law at Freiburg University, Federal Republic of Germany. Among his publications are *Die Geisteskrankheit in der Ehekonsenslehre Thomas Sanchez* (1971) and various articles for journals and works of reference.

$5.95

# CONCILIUM
## Religion in the Eighties

A multi-volume library of contemporary religious thought • published
in 10 volumes annually • exploring the
latest trends and developments in the Sociology of
Religion, Liturgy, Dogma, Practical Theology,
Fundamental Theology, Canon Law, Ecumenism,
Spirituality and Moral Theology

*Edited by*

GIUSEPPE ALBERIGO • JOSÉ LUIS ARANGUREN
GREGORY BAUM • LEONARDO BOFF
ANTOINE VAN DEN BOOGAARD • PAUL BRAND
LUCIANO CAGLIOTI • MARIE-DOMINIQUE CHENU O.P.
YVES CONGAR O.P. • MARIASUSAI DHAVAMONY S.J.
CHRISTIAN DUQUOC O.P. • AUGUST WILHELM VON EIFF
VIRGIL ELIZONDO • ELIZABETH SCHÜSSLER FIORENZA
CASIANO FLORISTAN • PAULO FREIRE
CLAUDE GEFFRÉ O.P. • ANDREW GREELEY
NORBERT GREINACHER • GUSTAVO GUITIÉRREZ MERINO
ANDRE HELLEGERS • PETER HUIZING S.J.
BAS VAN IERSEL S.M.M. • BARBARA WARD JACKSON
JEAN-PIERRE JOSSUA O.P. • HANS KÜNG
RENÉ LAURENTIN • LUIS MALDONADO
JOHANNES BAPTIST METZ • DIETMAR MIETH
JÜRGEN MOLTMANN • ALOIS MÜLLER
ROLAND MURPHY O. CARM • JACQUES MARIE POHIER O.P.
DAVID POWER O.M.I. • KARL RAHNER S.J.
JEAN REMY • LUIGI SARTORI
EDWARD SCHILLEBEECKX O.P. • DAVID TRACY
KNUT WALF • ANTON WEILER
HARALD WEINRICH • JOHN ZIZIOULAS

"A courageous and timely work. *Concilium* illumines the great issues of
today."
—*America*

"The most ambitious crash program ever undertaken in theological
re-education. The essays are uncompromisingly competent, solid, and
nourishing. *Concilium* is indispensable."
—*The Christian Century*

"A bold and confident venture in contemporary theology. All the best
new theologians are contributing to this collective summa."
—*Commonweal*

THE SEABURY PRESS, NEW YORK          T. & T. CLARK, EDINBURGH